Stenoscript ABC Shorthand

Revised Edition

Murlene Wallace Asadi

PARADIGM

Acquisition Editor Sharon L. Bouchard
Development Editor Kevin K. Neely
Composition & Design PC&F, Inc.
Proofreader Linda Purcell

The Stenoscript ABC Shorthand instructional program includes the textbook, *Student Transcript, Workbook, Dictionary, Dictation Text, Instructor's Guide and Test Bank, Learning Tape Library,* and *Learning Tape Library Transcript.*

Library of Congress Cataloging-in-Publication Data

Asadi, Murlene Wallace.
Stenoscript ABC shorthand

1. Shorthand—Stenoscript ABC. I. Title
Z56.2.S87A83 1989 653.42 89-6043
ISBN 1-56118-454-3 (previously 0-574-20110-6)

Printed in the United States of America

10 9 8 7 6 5 4

Contents

Introduction

THE SYSTEM

The shorthand system you will learn in this text is *Stenoscript ABC Shorthand.* The Stenoscript system is based on the letters of the alphabet and common punctuation symbols. Because it is easy to learn and easy to write, you can begin writing Stenoscript on the first day of instruction. You can master the entire theory of Stenoscript in a fraction of the time you would require to learn shorthand systems that are based on nonalphabetic symbols.

By regular, sustained practice, you will attain the speed needed for office dictation and various other notetaking situations. Many Stenoscript students have reached speeds of 80 to 100 words per minute. Furthermore, because Stenoscript uses no unusual or special symbols, your shorthand will be legible and easy to transcribe even months after you have written it. If necessary, your Stenoscript notes can also be quickly keyboarded on a typewriter or computer and transcribed later.

THE RULES

The Stenoscript ABC Shorthand system consists of 40 rules. These 40 rules can be briefly summarized into six general rules:

1. The symbols of Stenoscript are the letters of the alphabet, the slant mark, the dash, and the comma.
2. When you hear the *name* of a letter of the alphabet at the beginning or end of a word, write that letter. For example, in the sound of the word *easy*, you hear the two letters *e* and *z*, so you write *ez.*
3. Vowels are omitted except at the beginning and end of words or as noted in other rules.
4. Most long vowels that are followed by a final single consonant sound are retained. You will learn to recognize this long-vowel sound quickly.
5. The letters *l* and *r* are often left out of words.
6. Brief forms are memorized for words and sounds that occur frequently in the English language.

THE TEXT

The text presents the 40 Stenoscript rules individually. Each rule is followed by examples and additional practice words that are presented as Sound-Spelling Exercises and Application Exercises. At the end of each lesson, you are given a Comprehensive Word Review, additional Writing Exercises, and a series of Reading, Writing, and Transcription Exercises.

Sound-Spelling Exercises

Because Stenoscript is based on the way words sound, you must *hear* the words and exercises you are writing. When you are working from your book, *say* the words as you write them. If circumstances permit, say the words aloud. Otherwise, move your lips and pronounce the words mentally.

When you first begin to write in Stenoscript, you will be thinking about the sounds you are hearing and the Stenoscript outlines you are writing. You will be making a *conscious* association between sounds and symbols. As you practice and build skill, however, the sound-to-symbol process will become automatic and no longer require conscious effort. You will then begin to build your shorthand *speed.*

Application Exercises

The Application Exercises in each lesson list words that you are to write in Stenoscript by applying the particular rule that precedes the list. After completing the Application Exercise, check the accuracy of your Stenoscript outlines by consulting the answers in the *Student Transcript.* Be sure to rewrite any incorrect outlines. If you made an error in an outline that was presented in an earlier lesson, review the earlier rule and practice the Sound-Spelling Exercises that accompany that rule.

High-Frequency Words and Brief Forms

You must *memorize* the high-frequency words presented in Lessons 1–4 and the brief forms presented in Lesson 5. The high-frequency words and brief forms are the words and phrases that occur most often in English speech and writing. You will encounter them repeatedly in this text and in the dictation exercises given in class.

Comprehensive Word Review

The Comprehensive Word Review in each lesson is devoted to reinforcement and recall. It is designed to improve your understanding of the principles covered in the lesson and to strengthen the skills you developed in earlier lessons. It is also diagnostic; the words you miss in any part of the Comprehensive Word Review will tell you what rules you need to review and whether you need to spend more time memorizing the high-frequency words.

Reading, Writing, and Transcription Exercises

These exercises will sharpen your reading and transcription skills. Practice reading and writing these exercises until you can read the outlines without hesitation. Regardless of how perplexing it may seem standing alone, you will soon discover that the meaning of an outline becomes readily apparent in the context of a sentence or paragraph.

WRITING EFFICIENCY

Choosing a Pen

Select a good ballpoint pen. A ballpoint pen glides more easily on paper than a pencil or felt-tip pen, and you will be able to write faster and with less effort. Always have a spare pen available in case the first pen stops writing while you are taking dictation.

Your Shorthand Steno Pad

Use a standard stenographic note pad. Steno pads are spiral bound at the top so that pages can be turned easily. Each page of a steno pad is divided into two columns. Write on every line of your steno pad to the dividing line that runs down the center of the page. When you have finished writing on one side of a page, flip the page and continue writing on the next blank page. You can quickly locate blank pages in your steno pad by placing a rubber band around the used pages. After completing one side of your steno pad, turn it over and write on the reverse side of each page, from the back to the front.

To save time turning pages, slide each page upward as you write. When you finish the second column of the page, quickly flip the page over and continue writing on the top line of the next page. Do this even when you are not doing dictation exercises so that you will establish good habits from the first day of class.

If you make a mistake on an outline, strike out the error with a single stroke of your pen and write the correct outline.

Remember that *constant and sustained practice* is the key to your shorthand success!

HOW TO STUDY

Developing good study habits will enable you to reach your career goals. Although the Stenoscript system is easy to master, learning shorthand requires disciplined practice. The following study plan will help you use your time efficiently:

1. Study each rule and its sound-spelling exercise. As you sound out each word, think about how the rule applies to the word.
2. Complete the Application Exercise that follows each rule. First say the word aloud. Then sound-spell what you hear as you write the Stenoscript outline.
3. Check the accuracy of your Stenoscript outlines against the answers presented in the *Student Transcript.* If you wrote any outline incorrectly, practice writing the correct outline several times.
4. After completing the Application Exercises in the textbook, complete the supplementary exercises for that rule in the *Stenoscript ABC Shorthand Workbook.* These exercises will reinforce your understanding of the rules.
5. Check the accuracy of your work on the supplementary exercises against the Answer Key provided at the end of the *Stenoscript Workbook.* The Answer Key has been printed on perforated pages; remove these pages for quick and easy checking.
6. Complete the Comprehensive Word Review in the text. Check the accuracy of your outlines in the *Student Transcript.*
7. Complete the Reading, Writing, and Transcription Exercises as assigned by your instructor. These exercises will increase your ability to read Stenoscript outlines, sound out unfamiliar words, and transcribe Stenoscript notes quickly and accurately.

Punctuation Rules

As in all writing, correct punctuation is very important in writing and transcribing Stenoscript ABC Shorthand. As you write and transcribe the exercises in this text and the *Stenoscript ABC Shorthand Workbook*, use the following punctuation rules.

1. Ampersand

Use the ampersand when it is part of the official name of an organization.

Wilson & Sons   Albion Casters & Wheels

2. Apostrophe

Use the apostrophe

a. as a symbol for feet. (Inches are represented by quotation marks.)

5'   2' × 4'   9' by 12'   5'6"

b. as a symbol for hours. (Minutes are represented by quotation marks.)

3'   2'   3'45"

c. to indicate the omission of figures in dates.

graduate of '82   year '83   class of '84

d. to form contractions indicating the omission of letters.

I'd   I've   you'd   he'll   she's   doesn't

e. as a single quotation mark.

Note: A quotation within a quotation is enclosed in single quotation marks (see Rule 15a).

Peg said, "Art opened the sessions by saying, 'Welcome to the tenth annual Sports Banquet.'"

f. to form the plural of letters.

5 A's   I's   b's   j's   m's

g. to form possessives.

Betty's bike   David's desk   the company's profits

3. Asterisk

Use the asterisk

a. to refer the reader to a footnote.

Unemployment rates will decrease by 10 percent.*

---

*U.S. Department of Labor

b. to indicate the omission of paragraphs. Indicate the omission of paragraphs by three spaced asterisks with a double space before and after them.

* * *

4. Brackets

Use brackets

a. to indicate a *clarification, correction,* or *comment* in quoted material.

Clarification
"Cheryl asked the printer [Graphic Artists] to have the proofs ready by October 10."

Correction
He said, "I was going 55 miles an hour [police officer clocked him at 75 miles an hour] when the accident occurred."

Comment
"We forgot our tickets [laughter]; then we forgot the time."

b. to enclose the word *sic* (meaning *thus, so,* or *the way it was in the original*).

The travel broshure [*sic*] stated that accommodations were for two.

c. to indicate a parenthetical expression within a parenthetical expression.

(Arrival time [about 3 p.m.] was agreeable to all.)

5. Colon

Use a colon

a. after a complete sentence (a sentence containing a subject and predicate) that introduces lists or enumerations.

They require two identifications: a driver's license and a voter's registration card.

Note: Do not use a colon to separate a verb from its object or a preposition from its object.

Incorrect: The order includes: stationery, staples, and rubber stamps.
Correct: The order includes stationery, staples, and rubber stamps.

Incorrect: For more information write to: Dr. Harold Watson.
Correct: For more information write to Dr. Harold Watson.

Note: Generally, what precedes a colon should be a complete sentence.

b. before anticipatory expressions such as "these," "for example," "as follows," and "the following" when they introduce a list or series.

Please bring the following items: blankets, food, clothing, candles, and matches.

c. before an implied anticipatory expression.

The rule was simple: only four people in the viewing room at one time.

d. after salutations in business letters using mixed punctuation.

Ladies and Gentlemen:
Dear Ms. Holly:
Dear Mr. Battington:

e. to separate hours and minutes when time is expressed in figures.

8:30 9:45 1:15 4:30 5:15

f. to express ratios.

4:1 2:1

g. to separate titles and subtitles.

Communicating in Business: The Key to Success.

h. to separate the place of publication and the publisher in footnotes and bibliographies.

Chicago: Science Research Associates

i. to separate the volume number from the page number in footnotes and bibliographies.

5:125 25:384 1:89

6. Comma

The comma is the most frequently used—and misused—mark of punctuation. Use a comma

a. after introductory words, phrases, or clauses.

Fortunately, we had our reports with us.
About four o'clock in the morning, the telephone rang.
While you were out to lunch, Mr. Donahue called.

b. to separate three or more items in a series of words or phrases.

The secretary types, files, and answers the telephone.
Papers were on the desk, in the drawers, and on the floor.

c. to separate two independent clauses in a compound sentence when they are joined by a coordinating conjunction (*and, but, or, for, nor*).

The office manager reported to the vice-president, and the treasurer reported to the president.

d. to separate parenthetical and nonessential (nonrestrictive) words, phrases, and clauses that are unnecessary for the meaning of the sentence.

The house, which was built in 1906, has been remodeled.
The report, however, must be completed by the end of the month.
Sean O'Leary had a similar, though less costly, problem with his car.
Dr. Morgan, who will retire in two years, will serve as acting dean.

Note: Do not use commas to separate essential (restrictive) expressions. The italicized expressions in the following sentences are essential to the meaning of the sentence. If they were removed, the meaning of the sentence would be altered.

The house *that was built in 1906* has been remodeled. The other houses, however, have not been remodeled.

We *inadvertently* turned off the word processor. (We didn't mean to turn off the word processor; we did it unintentionally.)

The reporters *who were hired last year* will receive new assignments. (Not all reporters will receive new assignments, only those reporters who were hired last year.)

e. to set off nouns of direct address.

Dr. Burke, here are the files you requested.
Thank you, Ms. Franklin, for your donation.
That will be all for now, Jim.

f. to set off appositives (nouns or noun phrases that rename or explain a preceding noun or pronoun).

Our salesman, Tom Van Dyke, will demonstrate the Apple IIc.
One of our attorneys, a Notre Dame graduate, will be the speaker.

g. Do *not* use a comma to set off closely related appositives.

We secretaries agree with the resolution.

h. Do *not* use a comma to set off one-word appositives.

My sister Irene received her broker's license in 1975.

i. to set off a direct quotation.

"What time is the meeting," Bob asked, "and where will it be?"

j. to separate two or more adjectives that modify the same noun when the word *and* is appropriate but omitted.

Please use the enclosed, stamped envelope for your reply.

Note: Do *not* use a comma when the first adjective modifies the second adjective.

Sarah noted several glaring grammatical errors in the manuscript.

Note: Use a hyphen for compound adjectives when they precede a noun they modify. Do *not* use a hyphen when the compound adjectives follow the noun.

The well-known speaker received a standing ovation.
The speaker was well known.

k. before and after the day, date, and year. Do *not* use a comma when the date is expressed without the year or when the month and year are expressed without the date.

Our attorney will be here on Wednesday, August 10, 1990, to brief us.
The dedication of the new Byers Building will be November 2 at 2 p.m.
Plans for acquiring the property should be completed by May 1990.

l. to separate the elements within an address and to separate the city and the state. Do *not* use a comma to separate the state and zip code.

Please mail the package to Sue Williams, 702 Maple Road, Chicago, IL 60612, after September 5.

They plan to visit Detroit, Michigan, later this summer.

m. to set off abbreviations that follow a person's name.

Jerome Powers, Ph.D.
Denise Watts, D.D.S.
Cecil Mills, M.D.
Sister Anne Arnold, O.S.F.
Raymond Lloyd, Esq.

n. to separate an individual's first name from the last name when the name is given in inverted order.

O'Day, Jane   VanderRoest, Duane

o. to separate numbers into groups of thousands. Do *not* use commas to separate groups of thousands in years or policy, page, telephone, or serial numbers.

456,876	year 1983
policy number 2234590	page 1004
telephone 555-1121	serial number 4590453

p. to set off contrasting expressions.

Arthur, not Sam, will give the keynote address.

q. to indicate the omission of one or more words from a sentence when the omitted words are understood.

Two classes were added in accounting; three, in management.

r. to separate repeated words.

They worked very, very hard to accomplish the task.
When you work, work hard.

s. The modern tendency is to avoid using the comma to set off elements such as Jr., Sr., 2d, 3d, II, III, Inc., or Ltd.

George Price Jr.	Harold Schiedt III	John Seely 3d
Frost Inc.	Lloyd-Harris Ltd.	

7. Dash

The dash is formed by typing two consecutive hyphens without a space before, after, or between them. Use the dash

a. in place of other marks of punctuation for greater emphasis.

Three employees—Jill Harrison, Scott Homer, and Dan Boyd—will be promoted.

They forgot to include one important ingredient—milk.

Check Meijer's Market—on Westedge Avenue—before you make a decision.

b. before summarizing words.

Ribbons, thimbles, and diskettes—these are the items you'll need to purchase for your computer and printer.

The Powers, the Klines, and the Donaldsons—all have agreed to the sale.

c. after quotations and before the source.

"Every day in every way I'm getting better and better." —Emile Coué
"A stitch in time saves nine." —Anonymous

8. Slash

Use the slash

a. to write fractions.

$^3/_4$ $4\ ^5/_8$

b. for certain abbreviations and expressions.

and/or c/o

9. Ellipsis

Use the ellipsis (a series of three periods with a space before, between, and after each one) for emphasis in advertising or to show the omission of words from a quotation. When showing omissions, use a fourth period or other final mark of punctuation to indicate the end of a sentence.

You want to buy the computer that has all the necessary software . . . a speller . . . a graphics program . . . a math program . . . a word processing program.

"That's the point . . . !"

10. Exclamation Point

Use an exclamation point after a word, phrase, clause, or sentence to express strong feelings or emotions.

Oh! No! Sure! Stop it immediately!

11. Hyphen

Use a hyphen

a. in compound numerals from twenty-one to ninety-nine.

thirty-three fifty-eight eighty-seven

b. to identify numeric and alphabetic ranges.

pages 1–50 from A–Z

c. with the prefixes *self*, *ex*, and *great*.

self-contained ex-president great-grandmother

d. with a prefix and a root word that begins with a capital letter.

non-Western trans-American post-World War II days

e. between a prefix ending in *a* or *i* and a word beginning with the same letter.

anti-intellectual intra-atomic ultra-active semi-infinite

f. with the suffix *-elect*.

president-elect mayor-elect governor-elect

g. in compound adjectives when a noun follows.

well-organized report two-year plan up-to-date file

h. in spelled-out fractions.

one-third one-half three-quarters

i. in word divisions at the end of a line.

begin-ning busi-ness trans-por-ta-tion

12. Parentheses

Use parentheses

a. to set off nonessential elements. Commas and dashes may serve the same functions, but they can also *emphasize* essential elements, whereas parentheses *deemphasize*.

The store had a special sale on diskette (mini) desk files.

States with large electoral votes are California (4.5 million), Texas (2.98 million), and New York (10.7 million).

b. with references.

Pie charts (see Figure 12) divide a whole (100 percent) into segments.

c. with enumerated items.

The three main purposes of letters are to (1) inform, (2) inquire, and (3) persuade.

d. in outlines.

I.
  A.
    1.
      a.
        (1)
          (a)

13. Period

Use a period

a. at the end of a declarative sentence.

Auto dealers are giving big discounts in July and August.

b. at the end of an imperative command.

Turn off the lights when leaving the office.

c. after a polite request or command.

May I hear from you before June 10.

Please include a brochure with each of the letters.

d. after an indirect question.

The sales manager asked how many television sets were sold.

e. with abbreviations and initials.

Ms.	Mrs.	Mr.
Dr.	Rev.	Sr.
Ph.D.	c.o.d.	Co.
Inc.	J.T. Rax	M. Bartels

Note: When an abbreviation ends a sentence, do not add a second period.

The hikers were awake by 5 a.m. (*Not* a.m..)

Note: When an abbreviation ends an interrogative or exclamatory sentence, place the question mark or the exclamation point after the period.

Were the hikers awake by 5 a.m.?

Note: Omit periods in the call letters of most radio and television stations, government agencies, and various business and professional organizations. The modern tendency is to omit periods in all-capital abbreviations.

WKZO FICC YMCA AAUP AACSB IBM TRW

f. with amounts of money.

$25.35 $5 (Omit decimal and zeros in whole amounts.)

g. with percents.

5.5 percent 66.6 percent

h. with decimals.

2.5 10.75 23.108

i. for omissions and emphasis (see Rule 9).

j. after numbers or letters in an outline or list.

I.	1.
A.	2.
1.	3.
a.	4.

k. with headings.

Intimate Zone. The intimate zone covers the distance from touching to about 18 inches.

Personal Zone. The personal zone extends from about 18 inches to 4 feet.

Format: Space twice after a period at the end of a sentence. Space once after an initial or ending period in an abbreviation (E. L. Smith; 5:30 a.m. on Tuesday). Do *not* space between a decimal point and a number or after a period with an abbreviation (5.5, c.o.d.).

14. Question Mark

Use the question mark

a. to indicate a direct question.

What time will the meeting begin?

b. to indicate a question within a sentence.

You've heard, haven't you, that Larry Stobbe was appointed president?
You'll be able to attend, won't you?

c. to indicate a series of questions relating to the same subject and verb.

Shall we order hot dogs? hamburgers? fish sandwiches?

Note: Leave only one space after a question mark that appears within a sentence.

d. to indicate doubt.

Her diamond was 2.5 (?) carats.

15. Quotation Marks

Use quotation marks

a. to enclose direct quotations.

Commander Robert Crippen said, "What a way to come to California!"

Note: Use single quotation marks (apostrophes) to indicate a quotation within a quotation.

Marie said, "I said 'No' when Dorothy asked me."

Revert to double quotation marks (") for quoted material within the single-quoted material.

Mark said, "When Todd asked, 'Did you label the box "Fragile"?' I replied, 'No.'"

b. to enclose titles of articles, chapters, columns in newspapers and magazines, reports, manuscripts, unpublished dissertations, essays, short poems, songs, and radio and television programs.

Article:	"Challenger's Happy Landing"
Chapter:	"The Nature of Communication"
Column:	"National Affairs"
Song:	"The Star-Spangled Banner"
Television Program:	"60 Minutes"

c. to enclose expressions that are foreign, ungrammatical, humorous, slang or coined, or that need special emphasis.

When we arrived at the hotel, our friends had already prepared a "spread" on the bed.

The French term "vis-a-vis" means face-to-face.

Frances said Bill had the "guts" to do that kind of work.

d. to enclose words introduced by expressions such as "entitled," "marked," "labeled," and "signed."

The letters were marked "Confidential."

Placement: Periods and commas always go *inside* closing quotation marks. Semicolons and colons always go *outside* closing quotation marks.

"Profits increased 5 percent," the president said.

The president said, "Profits increased 5 percent."

He said, "I'll need a reply immediately"; however, it can be handwritten instead of typed.

A question mark or an exclamation point goes *inside* the closing quotation marks when it applies to the quoted material. It goes *outside* the closing quotation marks when it applies to the entire sentence.

Dr. Ralbadi asked, "Did you complete the manuscript?"
Where is the reprint of the article, "Nation at Risk"?

16. Semicolon

Use a semicolon

a. to separate independent clauses without using coordinating conjunctions (*and, but, or, for, nor, yet, so*).

The conclusions are objective statements based on the findings of the report; the recommendations are somewhat objective statements based on the conclusions.

b. before a transitional expression (*however, therefore, consequently*) that joins independent clauses. The expression is followed by a comma.

You may revise the letter of authorization; however, please keep the letter of transmittal as it is.

c. to prevent misreading when independent clauses are joined by a coordinating conjunction and one or both clauses contain internal commas.

  Yes, of course, I'll be able to complete the project by Friday, June 8, 1990; but I would like to have a letter from you, Mr. Ewing, stating the terms of our contract.

d. to separate items in a series when any of the items contains commas.

  Ms. Taylor planned to visit Seattle, Washington; Denver, Colorado; Chicago, Illinois; and Boston, Massachusetts.

17. Underscore

Note: To underscore words, use continuous lines with no breaks in the lines between words. Except for abbreviations that include periods, punctuation marks are not underlined.

Use an underscore

a. with titles of books, magazines, newspapers, pamphlets, long poems, movies, plays, musicals, paintings, and other literary and artistic works.

The Bible	Star Wars
Time	Oliver
The Wall Street Journal	The Night Watch

b. for special emphasis.

  It's not what you say but how you say it.

c. for words to be italicized in print.

  Titles should answer the five W questions: *who, what, when, where*, and *why*.

d. for words that are defined or referred to.

  The term sic means so, or "this is the way it was in the original."

LESSON

1

You will not need to change your basic handwriting style to write Stenoscript ABC Shorthand. You will, however, need to observe the following writing principles:

1. Speed is gained by *not* dotting the *j* or *i* or crossing the letter *t*.
2. Loop the small letter *s* so that it will not be confused with the comma, which is also a Stenoscript symbol.
3. To distinguish between the letters *t* and *l* and the letters *i* and *e*, be sure to close the *t* and *i* and to loop the *l* and *e*.
4. Streamline letters by eliminating tails and loops. Eliminating these extra strokes allows you to write your Stenoscript notes faster and more efficiently. Your writing will also be more legible and easier to read.

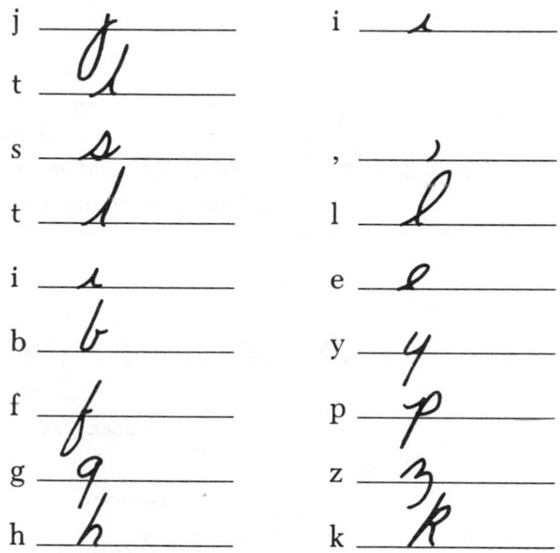

Rule 1a	*Write what you hear.*

In Stenoscript ABC Shorthand, you write only what you *hear.* This is called *sound-spelling.* For example, the word *pie* is written ____, and the word *knee* is written ____. This method of writing only what you hear will enable you to write your notes quickly and accurately.

SOUND-SPELLING EXERCISE

Sound-spell the following practice words and then write only what you hear. The sound-spelling guide next to each word will help you complete this exercise.

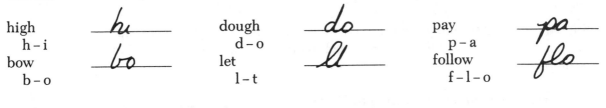

Word	Sound-spelling	Written
high	h – i	hi
bow	b – o	bo
dough	d – o	do
let	l – t	lt
pay	p – a	pa
follow	f – l – o	flo

Rule 1b	*Write vowel sounds* (a, e, i, o, u) *that occur at the beginning or end of a word. Do not write vowel sounds within a word.* (Exceptions will be noted in later lessons.)

SOUND-SPELLING EXERCISE

Word	Sound-spelling	Written
animal	a – n – m – l	anml
array	a – r – a	ara
borrow	b – r – o	bro
cab	k – b	Kb
cage	k – j	Kj
censor	s – n – s – r	snsr
cider	s – d – r	sdr
cipher	s – f – r	sfr
differ	d – f – r	dfr
item	i – t – m	itm
job	j – b	jb
law	l – a	la
give	g – v	gv
ledger	l – j – r	ljr
eager	e – g – r	egr
open	o – p – n	opn
ticket	t – k – t	tkt
unit	u – n – t	unt

APPLICATION EXERCISE

Applying the sound-spelling principles learned in Rules 1a and 1b, write the following words in Stenoscript. After completing the exercise, use the *Student Transcript* to check your work.

above ____________
a – b – v
amaze ____________
a – m – z
auto ____________
a – t – o
back ____________
b – k
because ____________
b – k – z
bitten ____________
b – t – n
book ____________
b – k
bottom ____________
b – t – m
cancel ____________
k – n – s – l
cater ____________
k – t – r
cigar ____________
s – g – r
damage ____________
d – m – j
egg ____________
e – g
error ____________
e – r – r
favor ____________
f – v – r
fellow ____________
f – l – o
few ____________
f – u

good ____________
g – d
judge ____________
j – j
level ____________
l – v – l
matter ____________
m – t – r
maze ____________
m – z
metal ____________
m – t – l
newspaper ____________
n – z – p – p – r
notice ____________
n – t – s
package ____________
p – k – j
pie ____________
p – i
recess ____________
r – s – s
review ____________
r – v – u
rose ____________
r – z
sell ____________
s – l
size ____________
s – z
some ____________
s – m

In the words *few* and *review,* notice that *u* is used for the long-vowel sounds of *oo* and *u.* Also notice that *book* and *back* are written exactly the same way. These are only two of the many words that are written exactly the same in Stenoscript ABC Shorthand. When you are transcribing actual dictation, however, you can determine the correct word from the *context of the sentence* in which it is used, as shown in these examples:

Put the __bk__ on the table.

Put it __bk__ on the table.

Rule 2	***When the initial or final sound of a word is the name of a letter of the alphabet, write that letter.*** (The following letters have an *e* sound: *b, c, d, g, p, t, v,* and *z.* When writing a word that ends in one of these letters, it is not necessary to write the final *e* sound.) ***Remember, do not write vowel sounds within a word.***

SOUND-SPELLING EXERCISE

Word	Sounds	Shorthand
argue	r – g – u	rgu
arm	r – m	rm
away	a – w – a	awa
baby	b – b	bb
easy	e – z	ez
else	l – s	ls
enemy	n – m – e	nme
icy	i – c	ic
key	k – e	ke
melody	m – l – d	mld
repay	r – p – a	rpa
sunny	s – n – e	sne

APPLICATION EXERCISE

Word	Sounds	Shorthand
candy	k – n – d	________
city	s – t	________
encourage	n – k – r – j	________
fancy	f – n – c	________
funny	f – n – e	________
happy	h – p	________
heavy	h – v	________
honey	h – n – e	________
ivy	i – v	________
money	m – n – e	________
regency	r – j – n – c	________
wise	y – z	________

Rule 3	*When a base word ends in a double consonant sound, write the first of the two sounds.* (Other rules involving consonants take precedence over this rule.)

SOUND-SPELLING EXERCISE

adopt a – d – p	adp	expect x – p – k	xpk	task t – s	ts
direct d – r – k	drk	loft l – f	lf	text t – x	tx

APPLICATION EXERCISE

desk d – s	______	except x – s – p	______	next n – x	______
detect d – t – k	______	fact f – k	______	object o – b – j – k	______
eject e – j – k	______	left l – f	______	soft s – f	______

Rule 4	*Whenever* d *or* ed *(pronounced* ed *or* duh*) is added to a base word, underline the last letter or symbol.*

SOUND-SPELLING EXERCISE

adopted a – d – p – ed	ad<u>p</u>	borrowed b – r – o – duh	br<u>o</u>
detected d – t – k – ed	dt<u>k</u>	fixed f – x – duh	f<u>x</u>

APPLICATION EXERCISE

accepted a – k – s – p – ed	______	caused k – z – duh	______
amazed a – m – z – duh	______	damaged d – m – j – duh	______
catered k – t – r – duh	______	defied d – f – i – duh	______

(continued)

directed d – r – k – ed	________	reviewed r – v – u – duh	________
objected o – b – j – k – ed	________		

Rule 5	*A plural word ending in* s *or* es *is written with a dot under the last letter or symbol in the word. Verbs that form their third-person singular by adding* s *or* es *also have dots.*

SOUND-SPELLING EXERCISE

animals a – n – m – l – s	amml.	cigars s – g – r – s	sgr.
cabs k – b – s	kb.	packages p – k – j – s	pkj.

Remember that verbs that form their third-person singular forms by adding *s* or *es* also have dots.

borrows b – r – o – s	bro.	runs r – n – s	rn.
pays p – a – s	pa.	sells s – l – s	sl.

APPLICATION EXERCISE

books b – k – s	________	newspapers n – z – p – p – r – s	________
eggs e – g – s	________	reviews r – v – u – s	________

Rule 6	*Use the special Stenoscript marks to indicate a period, question mark, comma, parentheses, hyphen, dash, new paragraph, or capitalization.*

period	\	hyphen	=
question mark	?	dash	==
parentheses	( )	comma	)

To indicate a new paragraph, use two long slant marks and then continue writing on the same line.

New paragraph	//

To indicate capitalization, place tick marks under the last letter or symbol in the word.

Betty b – t	bt	American a – m – r – k – n	amrkn
Roger r – j – r	rjr	IBM i – b – m	ibm

Rule 7a	*You may use any common abbreviation that is shorter than the Stenoscript outline.*

For example, since the standard abbreviation for *manager* is shorter than the Stenoscript outline, you may prefer to use the standard abbreviation.

Stenoscript Outline		*Common Abbreviation*	
manager m – n – j – r	mnjr	manager m – g – r	mgr

Rule 7b	*Write figures for numbers. Use the special Stenoscript abbreviations, however, for very large rounded numbers.*

Number	***Special Abbreviation***
hundred	h
thousand	t
million	m
billion	b

Examples:

500	5h	five	5
600,000	6hl	8,000	8l
9,000,000,000	9b	2,000,000	2m

MONEY AMOUNTS

Write money amounts as follows:

\$16.95	16^{95}	\$9,000,000	9m\$	\$700,000	7hl\$
\$700	7h\$	\$6,000	6l\$	five cents	5¢

Notice that monetary figures are written with the dollar or cent sign *after* the number. Also notice that the dollar sign has only one line through it.

Rule 8	***Memorize the Stenoscript outlines of the high-frequency words.***

Approximately 120 words occur with great frequency in written and spoken English. These words are called *high-frequency words* and are an important part of any shorthand system. The high-frequency words can be written quickly and will greatly increase your Stenoscript speed. The high-frequency words have been divided into four groups so that they can be easily memorized. The first group appears in this lesson. The other groups appear in Lessons 2, 3, and 4.

MEMORIZATION TIP

Since the high-frequency words are so important to writing Stenoscript successfully, the following memorization tip will be especially helpful. Memorize the words in two different ways. First, memorize the symbol used for each word. Then use the symbol to memorize all the words for that symbol. To recall these words instantly requires frequent, repetitive practice.

Memorize the Symbol	
be	b
been	b
being	b
by	b
bye	b
buy	b
but	b

Memorize the Words

b {
- be
- been
- being
- by
- bye
- buy
- but

HIGH-FREQUENCY WORDS: GROUP 1

a an	a
and	&
be been being by bye buy but	b
see seen seeing	c
says	sz
do due did done doing	d
day	D
does	dz
he me	e
for	f
go gone going	g
goes	gz
had have having	h
has	hz
I	I
if is it its	i
came can come coming	k

QUICK COMMA REVIEW

Complete punctuation rules are presented at the front of the book. Because the comma is the most frequently used punctuation mark, we will review some of the rules for comma usage in each lesson of the book. Use a comma

a. after introductory words, phrases, or clauses.

> Fortunately, we had our reports with us.
> About four o'clock in the morning, the telephone rang.
> While you were out to lunch, Mr. Donahue called.

b. to separate three or more items in a series of words or phrases.

> The secretary types, files, and answers the telephone.
> Papers were on the desk, in the drawers, and on the floor.

COMPREHENSIVE WORD REVIEW

Check your progress by writing Stenoscript outlines in your steno pad for the following words:

1. adopt
2. coming
3. get
4. having
5. review
6. package
7. some
8. next
9. me
10. autos
11. cipher
12. he
13. level
14. judge
15. but
16. manager
17. due
18. damaged
19. animal
20. have
21. eject
22. be
23. pie
24. see
25. differ
26. buy
27. fact
28. eye
29. came
30. did
31. maze
32. caged
33. eggs
34. it
35. and
36. gone
37. for
38. has
39. fixed
40. if
41. censor
42. goes
43. regency
44. done
45. object
46. catered
47. been
48. a
49. amazed
50. back
51. city
52. seeing
53. day
54. roses

WRITING EXERCISE

Practice writing these sentences in Stenoscript in your steno pad:

1. I have a book. It is a good book, but I have had a better book.
2. It is an easy task, and I can do it.
3. He is having it fixed.
4. Did he get a package?
5. He came for me, but I had gone.
6. See if he has some roses I can buy.
7. He left me a ticket, but I have one.
8. I have seen a funny metal object.
9. I recall seeing some tickets and a package.
10. If I see a good book, I can buy it.

READING, WRITING, AND TRANSCRIPTION EXERCISES

After studying only the first eight rules in Stenoscript, you can now read, write, and transcribe shorthand notes.

The following exercises are especially designed to strengthen your shorthand skills. By reading the following exercises, you can improve your reading skills. When possible, read these exercises aloud. If you encounter a word that you cannot read, sound-spell the word. If you still cannot read the word, continue reading to the end of the sentence. The meaning of the sentence may help you figure out the outline. If you still cannot read the outline, consult your *Student Transcript* for the correct word.

Your instructor may ask you to transcribe one or more of these exercises in class. As you transcribe the exercises, you will need to insert the correct punctuation marks (commas, colons, periods, etc.). If you are unsure about the use of punctuation, consult the Punctuation Rules in the front of this book. If you need further explanation of some punctuation rules, ask your instructor for assistance. As you gain confidence, you will be able to apply the correct punctuation automatically during dictation and transcription tests.

These exercises may also be used to time your reading rate, or they may be given as supplementary writing assignments.

READING, WRITING, AND TRANSCRIPTION EXERCISES

(1)

I K uz a pnsl.
e K b e a pnsl.
I K uz a pn. i
e gz c i e K gl
e a pn. c i e
K b e sm ppr
wn e gl m a pn.
i e gl e a pnsl
a pn & sm ppr I
K pa f i.

(2)

e hz a dg. i i a bg
dg. i i i a gd dg
e K b i sm lvr.
i i i a bd dg e
K sl i. i I c a
gd dg I pl i. i
I c a bd dg I
rn.

(3)

I h a kr. i i a
gd kr wn i rn.
i hz a gd mtr.
i i gz bd I K h
i fx. i e b i e
K pa e f i. i I
c a btr kr I K b
i. I h sm mne
& I K pa f i.

LESSON 2

Lesson 2 presents Stenoscript Rules 9 through 16, High-Frequency Words Group 2, and appropriate exercises.

Rule 9	*When you hear the* ch *sound, write a small* c.

SOUND-SPELLING EXERCISE

attach a – t – ch	alc	catch k – ch	kc
teacher t – ch – r	tcr	chop ch – p	cp

APPLICATION EXERCISE

choose ch – z	________	kitchen k – ch – n	________	such s – ch	________
coach k – ch	________	much m – ch	________	teach t – ch	________
detach d – t – ch	________	reach r – ch	________	watch w – ch	________

Rule 10	*Use a dash (—) to represent the word* the *and the* th *(pronounced* ith*),* nd, nt, mand, mend, *and* ment *sounds. Connect the dash to the letter preceding or following it in the word.*

SOUND-SPELLING EXERCISE

a. The *th* (pronounced *ith*) sound

bath b – ith	b—	other o – ith – r	o—r	then ith – n	—n

APPLICATION EXERCISE

a. The *th* (pronounced *ith*) sound

beneath ____________
  b – n – ith
both ____________
  b – ith
death ____________
  d – ith
either ____________
  e – ith – r

father ____________
  f – ith – r
feather ____________
  f – ith – r
gather ____________
  g – ith – r
leather ____________
  l – ith – r

than ____________
  ith – n
that ____________
  ith – t
their ____________
  ith – r
them ____________
  ith – m

SOUND-SPELLING EXERCISE

b. The *nd, nt, mand, mend,* and *ment* sounds

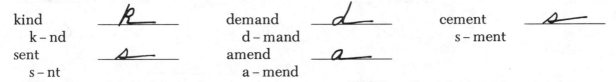

kind 
  k – nd
sent 
  s – nt

demand 
  d – mand
amend 
  a – mend

cement 
  s – ment

APPLICATION EXERCISE

b. The *nd, nt, mand, mend,* and *ment* sounds

account ____________
  a – k – nt
attend ____________
  a – t – nd
event ____________
  e – v – nt
evident ____________
  e – v – d – nt
expand ____________
  x – p – nd
extend ____________
  x – t – nd

tent ____________
  t – nt
patent ____________
  p – t – nt
resident ____________
  r – z – d – nt
round ____________
  r – nd
sound ____________
  s – nd
want ____________
  w – nt

SOUND-SPELLING EXERCISE

c. If a word requires two adjoining dashes, connect the two dashes with a slight jog. The jog will look like the small letter *z*.

amendment a - mend - ment	a—

APPLICATION EXERCISE

c. Two adjoining dashes

attendant a - t - nd - nt	________	descendant d - s - nd - nt	________
defendant d - f - nd - nt	________	pendant p - nd - nt	________
dependent d - p - nd - nt	________	redundant r - d - nd - nt	________

You have learned to drop vowels within words when writing Stenoscript outlines. When adding word endings, however, always write the final base-word vowel.

Base Word		*Word Ending*	
rely r - l - i	rli	reliant r - l - i - nt	rli—
pay p - a	pa	payment p - a - ment	pa—

Rule 11	*When you hear the* ng *sound, write a small* g.

SOUND-SPELLING EXERCISE

among a - m - ng	amg	angle a - ng - l	agl	eating e - t - ng	elg

APPLICATION EXERCISE

along ____________
a – l – ng

backing ____________
b – k – ng

boxing ____________
b – x – ng

chopping ____________
ch – p – ng

demanding ____________
d – mand – ng

hanging ____________
h – ng – ng

hung ____________
h – ng

judging ____________
j – j – ng

longing ____________
l – ng – ng

paying ____________
p – a – ng

saying ____________
s – a – ng

selling ____________
s – l – ng

single ____________
s – ng – l

something ____________
s – m – ith – ng

wrong ____________
r – ng

Did you write the base-word vowel when adding word endings to *paying* and *saying*?

Rule 12	*When you hear the* shun, chun, *or* zhun *sound, write a small* j.

SOUND-SPELLING EXERCISE

action 
a – k – shun

fashion 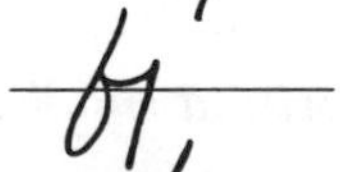
f – shun

attention 
a – t – n – shun

occasion 
o – k – zhun

digestion 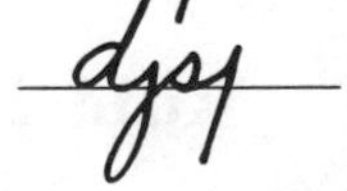
d – j – s – chun

APPLICATION EXERCISE

definition ______
  d – f – n – shun
edition ______
  e – d – shun
location ______
  l – k – shun
mention ______
  m – n – shun
motion ______
  m – shun
nation ______
  n – shun
reception ______
  r – s – p shun

position ______
  p – z – shun
section ______
  s – k – shun
selection ______
  s – l – k – shun
session ______
  s – shun
objection ______
  o – b – j – k – shun
vision ______
  v – zhun
vocation ______
  v – k – shun

Rule 13	*When you hear the* sh *(prounounced* ish*) or* zh *sound, write a small* z.

SOUND-SPELLING EXERCISE

fish fz
  f – ish
issue izu
  i – ish – u

measure mzr
  m – zh – r
patient pz
  p – ish – nt

ship zp
  ish – p

APPLICATION EXERCISE

ancient ______
  a – n – ish – nt
cash ______
  k – ish
deficient ______
  d – f – ish – nt
diminish ______
  d – m – n – ish

dish ______
  d – ish
lash ______
  l – ish
leash ______
  l – ish
leisure ______
  l – zh – r

(continued)

push ______
  p – ish
rush ______
  r – ish
shell ______
  ish – l
shoe ______
  ish – u

shop ______
  ish – p
show ______
  ish – o
wish ______
  w – ish

Rule 14	*When you hear the* nk *(pronounced* ink*) or* qu *(pronounced* kw*) sound, write a small* q.

SOUND-SPELLING EXERCISE

a. The *nk* (pronounced *ink*) sound

bank bq
  b – nk

link lq
  l – nk

b. The *qu* (pronounced *kw*) sound

equal eql
  e – kw – l

quit ql
  kw – t

APPLICATION EXERCISE

function ______
  f – nk – shun
rank ______
  r – nk
sink ______
  c – nk
thank ______
  ith – nk
think ______
  ith – nk
wrinkle ______
  r – nk – l

acquit ______
  a – kw – t
liquid ______
  l – kw – d
qualify ______
  kw – l – f – i
quiver ______
  kw – v – r
quiz ______
  kw – z
sequel ______
  c – kw – l

Rule 15	*Write the letter* l *if it is doubled* (ll) *or if it occurs between two vowels within a base word. Otherwise, omit the* l.

SOUND-SPELLING EXERCISE

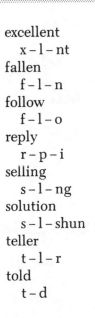

application a – p – k – shun	apkj	
blank b – nk	bq	
block b – k	bk	
blue b – u	bu	
bullet b – l – t	bll	
called k – l – duh	Kl	
children ch – d – n	cdn	
clever k – v – r	Kvr	
excellent x – l – nt	xl	
fallen f – l – n	fln	
follow f – l – o	flo	
reply r – p – i	rpi	
selling s – l – ng	slg	
solution s – l – shun	slj	
teller t – l – r	tlr	
told t – d	td	

APPLICATION EXERCISE

belong ________
b – l – ng

black ________
b – k

blow ________
b – o

cellar ________
s – l – r

clinic ________
k – n – k

color ________
k – l – r

delay ________
d – l – a

deliver ________
d – l – v – r

develop ________
d – v – l – p

dollar ________
d – l – r

fellow ________
f – l – o

flush ________
f – ish

glass ________
g – s

gold ________
g – d

hollow ________
h – l – o

pillow ________
p – l – o

pilot ________
p – l – t

plan ________
p – n

play ________
p – a

regular ________
r – g – l – r

sell ________
s – l

sold ________
s – d

solid ________
s – l – d

Rule 16	*Write the letter* r *if it is doubled* (rr) *or if it occurs between two vowels within a base word. Otherwise, omit the* r.

SOUND-SPELLING EXERCISE

attorney
a – t – n – e ___alne___
borrow
b – r – o ___bro___
dress
d – s ___ds___
endorse
n – d – s ___nds___
farmer
f – m – r ___fmr___
furrow
f – r – o ___fro___
perfect
p – f – k ___pfk___
president
p – z – d – nt ___pzd___
pretend
p – t – nd ___pt___
professor
p – f – s – r ___pfsr___

APPLICATION EXERCISE

bring ___________
b – ng
brother ___________
b – ith – r
caress ___________
k – r – s
carriage ___________
k – r – j
carrot ___________
k – r – t
chorus ___________
k – r – s
courage ___________
k – r – j
critic ___________
k – t – k
cross ___________
k – s
current ___________
k – r – nt
enrich ___________
n – r – ch
forbid ___________
f – b – d
forget ___________
f – g – t
former ___________
f – m – r
hero ___________
h – r – o
merit ___________
m – r – t
oral ___________
o – r – l
parent ___________
p – r – nt
product ___________
p – d – k
promise ___________
p – m – s
protect ___________
p – t – k
purchase ___________
p – ch – s
purse ___________
p – s
quarrel ___________
kw – r – l
rural ___________
r – r – l
series ___________
s – r – z
service ___________
s – v – s
sorrow ___________
s – r – o
traffic ___________
t – f – k
truck ___________
t – k

HIGH-FREQUENCY WORDS: GROUP 2

Words	Symbol
all well will	l
answer	a
however	H
mine my am him many	m
month	M
in neither know no none nor not	n
or on owe so	o
out	O
up	p
question	Q
are her hers our ours hour	r
saw us	s
at to too	t
the	—

HIGH-FREQUENCY WORD REVIEW

Write the high-frequency words for the following Stenoscript symbols:

d ____________
____
____
____
____

b ____________
____
____
____
____
____
____

e ____________
____

gz ____________

dz ____________

f ____________

(continued)

i	________	sz	________	h	________
	________	k	________		________
	________		________		________
	________		________		
c	________		________		
	________	a	________		
	________		________		

CONFUSING WORDS

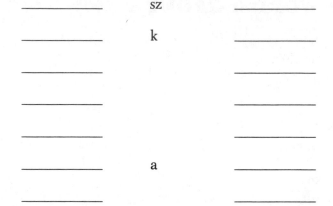

Because many words have similar sounds, they are often misspelled and misused. Learning the proper use of these words will enable you to transcribe your Stenoscript notes quickly and accurately.

Notice how these commonly misspelled and misused words are used in the following examples:

Word	***Definition***
their	possessive
there	in or at that place
they're	they are

Their shorthand books will arrive tomorrow.
There are 21 students in our shorthand class.
They're planning to attend the business conference.

QUICK COMMA REVIEW

Recalling the punctuation rules at the front of the book, remember to use a comma

c. to separate two independent clauses in a compound sentence when they are joined by a coordinating conjunction (*and, but, or, for, nor*).

The office manager reported to the vice-president, and the treasurer reported to the president.

d. to separate parenthetical and nonessential (nonrestrictive) words, phrases, and clauses that are unnecessary for the meaning of the sentence.

The house, which was built in 1906, has been remodeled.
The report, however, must be completed by the end of the month.
Sean O'Leary had a similar, though less costly, problem with his car.
Dr. Morgan, who will retire in two years, will serve as acting dean.

Note: Do not use commas to separate essential (restrictive) expressions. The italicized expressions in the following sentences are essential to the meaning of the sentence. If they were removed, the meaning of the sentence would be altered.

The house *that was built in 1906* has been remodeled. The other houses, however, have not been remodeled.

We *inadvertently* turned off the word processor. (We didn't mean to turn off the word processor; we did it unintentionally.)

The reporters *who were hired last year* will receive new assignments. (Not all reporters will receive new assignments, only those reporters who were hired last year.)

COMPREHENSIVE WORD REVIEW

Check your progress by writing Stenoscript outlines in your steno pad for the following words:

1. eager
2. else
3. sounded
4. will
5. recess
6. happy
7. tent
8. well
9. judge
10. agency
11. payments
12. all
13. some
14. detect
15. finding
16. none
17. have
18. desk
19. something
20. not
21. can
22. runs
23. scction
24. nor
25. be
26. catch
27. education
28. neither
29. goes
30. much
31. possession
32. know
33. come
34. the
35. fishing
36. no
37. if
38. death
39. quiet
40. in
41. issue
42. back
43. favor
44. him
45. notice
46. sell
47. forget
48. many

(continued)

49. cross	57. play	65. product
50. alarmed	58. accounts	66. thank
51. shoe	59. service	67. at
52. am	60. crew	68. us
53. leather	61. quick	69. them
54. blank	62. glass	70. bent
55. watched	63. blue	71. argue
56. my	64. helps	72. caress

WRITING EXERCISE

Practice writing these sentences in Stenoscript in your steno pad:

1. He can reach the chopped wood.
2. If he is talking, I can pay the check.
3. The older hotel has excellent service.
4. I showed her my matchbook cover collection.
5. The metal box is bigger and better than the wooden box.
6. The teacher told me to go to the office for the book.
7. This lesson is easy, but you have to pay attention.
8. I think that I am going to the carnival.
9. Show me a quick way to get this done.
10. The payment came this morning.

READING, WRITING, AND TRANSCRIPTION EXERCISES

(1)

e ld e l b l —
bk. e sd —l e wd
pa e. —d n —l e
pa — bl f — bk
ak.

(2)

— kc cz — mn
& lc —m l pa bl.
—a ln l kc & l
—o & l rn l. —a
d n ms pkls bkz
—a w— l ln l pa
blr. — kc ll —m
—l i —a pkls l
—a l wn.

(3)

—d —q — ofs i b
mnj l. — mn
—l rn — ofs f
e i a sl— mnjr.
— nu mn l ln
— jb i e obzv
— mnjr. —d l
q w— m i —d k.
i wd b a gd wa
f e l c i —q r
q l.

(4)

— mn hz a nu
lcq pzj. e lc n
— bdg —a opn n
— fl. e dz — jb
l bkz e i a gd
lcr. e i n hz b
e i fm & — ks
rspk m. f —s
rzn e i rspk b
— m r & f r l.
— ppl e lc l
gl a gd ejkj. —
o r pr. wz —r

cdn Kd b n —l
Ks.

(5)

ppl fm m nj K
l r l— l lv.
—a K f m dfr
ryn b —a h l
ryn n jnrl. —a
K bkz —a r lkq f
a blr wa l lv.
i i n lwz ez
bkz —a h mc l
ln b wn —a bk
slyn —a r hp.

(6)

i u b a uz Kr c
i i hz b dmj. i
i hz b dmj + —
dmj hz lrd b fx
i ma n b ez l
dlk. a gd Kr ajnc
l ll u —l —
Kr hz b dmj.

—a l ll u wl
—a h d l fx
— dmj. — uz
Kr u b ma n b
gd i — ajnc slq
i i n gd. a ajnc
—l dz n ll u—
—l K Kz u m
spnsv pbm. ll i
u h l bro l b a
Kr lk f gd lm.
c wl lm — ajnc
l gv u. c wl lm
u K gl l a bq.
u h l cz lm —l
r gd f u. i i n
ez l jj z mbr wn
l u w— l d i gl
n— Kr + dv i.
b wl u d wn u r
bq a Kr l e r hp
u o kz pbm n —
fcr. ll wn u b a

uz Kr f— a gd
ajnc. gl lm u K
hl & u l h ng
l rgl. u l b hp
w— sc a pcs.

(7)

i i l f a fm l
arny f Klkg i
bl. i a ak— k d
& n pa— i rcv a
sml fm ma n
h — Kz i hz l
h l pa i bl & gl
nu pdk rd. i
hz l h sm Kz
n h— i i i l ofr
nu pdk & svs. i
hz l h a gd pn f
Klkg i bl.// an r
pbm a fm ma h i
idl hp. i a fm hz
a Ku —l i n bz
— wy f —o idl

Ku r sp— l n
pps. a fm Kn
gl nu hp f ec nu
jb. i hz l h a
bsk Ku o i K d jb
wn —a K n. i i
n ez f a fm l gl
hp l al— l jb n
pn f. H i a Ku
i Kp o h— a fx
mne O9 i nvv.
— Ku hz l b pa.
—o i a pbm —l
hz l b pn f l.
i i a dfKl pbm.

(8)

— fm dlvr i Kr—
pdk n lk. bkz i
br r n — ara i
dz n uz o r svs.
H uzq i on lk hz
Kz sm pbm// i
bq pbm — fm hz

i glg a gd lk Ku.
glg dvr l dv l & l
b rglr o — jb i
dfkl. n adj wn
u gl dvr —a h l
b ll l h—l gd.
nx —a h l ln l
lk l K—. a
mn K b gd l pkg
a lk & h—lg gd &
n b gd l lkg l
ppl. o e ma n
b gd l h—lg —
dk— —l h l b fl
O. ll c l i —l—
lk r lvz rng l i
an—r bg pbm. a fm
—l dz i on lkg
lvz hz l h mknk
o a svs arnj— w
an—r fm. — wa
—s pbm i h—l i
dlmn b — xp—cr

i nvr. 1 slj l
ln O l b ls xpnsv
—n an—r f a gvn
fm. ll l sv —r dvr
pbm. m fm b —
svs —a w—. —r
r sm fm —l d
nq b lkg. z fm
h dvr mknk + lk
rd l ofr l o—r fm
f a fe. bkz —a
sl —r svs l m
fm lkg fm K en
mne l pcs m lk.
— dvr —a uz H
l h rglr jb.

LESSON 3

Lesson 3 presents Stenoscript Rules 17 through 21, Stenoscript outlines for city and state names, High-Frequency Words Group 3, and appropriate exercises.

Rule 17	***Use a slant mark (/) to represent the* rd, rt, *and* rk *sounds and the letter group* ward.**

SOUND-SPELLING EXERCISE

a. The *rd* sound

accord
  a – k – rd

guard
  g – rd

harder
  h – rd – r

order
  o – rd – r
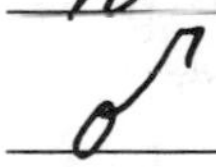

Notice that when the slant is used within a word, as in *harder* and *order*, you continue writing at the top of the slant.

APPLICATION EXERCISE

a. The *rd* sound

afford a – f – rd	________	cards k – rd – s	________	record r – k – rd	________
bird b – rd	________	garden g – rd – n	________	regard r – g – rd	________
board b – rd	________	hard h – rd	________	yard y – rd	________
burden b – rd – n	________	pardon p – rd – n	________	word w – rd	________

SOUND-SPELLING EXERCISE

b. The *rt* sound

alert 
a – l – rt

apartment 
a – p – rt – ment

effort 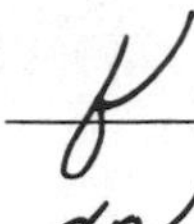
f – rt

exported 
x – p – rt – ed

APPLICATION EXERCISE

b. The *rt* sound

assert ___________
a – s – rt

court ___________
k – rt

department ___________
d – p – rt – ment

deport ___________
d – p – rt

expert ___________
x – p – rt

hurt ___________
h – rt

mortal ___________
m – rt – l

quarter ___________
kw – rt – r

reported ___________
r – p – rt – ed

reverted ___________
r – v – rt – ed

sorted ___________
s – rt – ed

supported ___________
s – p – rt – ed

SOUND-SPELLING EXERCISE

c. The *rk* sound

dark 
d – rk

marking 
m – rk – ng

APPLICATION EXERCISE

c. The *rk* sound

clerk ___________
k – rk

network ___________
n – t – w – rk

park ___________
p – rk

remarking ___________
r – m – rk – ng

sparkle
s – p – rk – l ________

turkey
t – rk – e ________

work
w – rk ________

working
w – rk – ng ________

SOUND-SPELLING EXERCISE

d. The *ward* letter group

backward
b – k – ward bk/

warden
ward – n /n

outward
out – ward o/

APPLICATION EXERCISE

d. The *ward* letter group

awarding
a – ward – ng ________

forward
for – ward ________

inward
in – ward ________

rewarding
r – ward – ng ________

upward
up – ward ________

wayward
w – a – ward ________

Rule 18	***When you hear the* ry *or* rry *(pronounced* ree*) letter group at the end of a word or the* oi *sound, write a small* y.**

SOUND-SPELLING EXERCISE

a. The *ry* and *rry* (pronounced *ree*) letter groups

battery
b – t – ree bly

century
s – n – ch – ree sncy

injury
n – j – ree njy

sorry
s – ree sy

APPLICATION EXERCISE

a. The *ry* and *rry* (pronounced *ree*) letter groups

carry ________
k – ree

dairy ________
d – ree

delivery ________
d – l – v – ree

grocery ________
g – s – ree

hurry ________
h – ree

jury ________
j – ree

luxury ________
l – k – zh – ree

misery ________
m – z – ree

salary ________
s – l – ree

summary ________
s – m – ree

voluntary ________
v – l – n – t – ree

worry ________
w – ree

SOUND-SPELLING EXERCISE

b. The *oi* sound

annoy any
a – n – oi

choice cys
ch – oi – s

employed mpy-
m – p – oi – ed

point py
p – oi – nt

APPLICATION EXERCISE

b. The *oi* sound

appoint ________
a – p – oi – nt

boy ________
b – oi

coin ________
k – oi – n

enjoyed ________
n – j – oi – duh

foil ________
f – oi – l

invoice ________
n – v – oi – s

joined ________
j – oi – n – duh

joint ________
j – oi – nt

loyal ________
l – oi – l

royal ________
r – oi – l

soil ________
s – oi – l

voice ________
v – oi – s

Rule 19	When you hear the mis *or* im *sound at the beginning of a word, write a small* m. *For words that begin* imm, *however, write* im.

SOUND-SPELLING EXERCISE

a. The *mis* sound

misfit mis – f – t	mfl	misspend mis – s – p – nd	msp
misuse mis – u – z (*v*)	muz	misuse mis – u – s (*n*)	mus

Notice that when *mis* is added to a word that begins with a vowel sound, as in *misuse*, you must write the vowel of the base word.

APPLICATION EXERCISE

a. The *mis* sound

misapply mis – a – p – i	________	mishandle mis – h – nd – l	________
misbehave mis – b – h – v	________	mishap mis – h – p	________
misbrand mis – b – nd	________	misjudge mis – j – j	________
miscount mis – k – nt	________	mislay mis – l – a	________
misdirect mis – d – r – k	________	mismatch mis – m – ch	________
misgiving mis – g – v – ng	________	misspell mis – s – p – l	________

SOUND-SPELLING EXERCISE

b. The *im* sound

image im – j	mj	impress m – p – s	mps

(continued)

impeach mpc
m – p – ch
impend mp–
m – p – nd
impersonal mpsnl
m – p – s – n – l
imported mp-
m – p – rt – ed
imbed mbd
m – b – d
impulsive mpsv
m – p – s – v

APPLICATION EXERCISE

b. The *im* sound

imagination ____________
im – j – n – shun
imagine ____________
im – j – n
imitation ____________
im – t – shun
impact ____________
im – p – k
impel ____________
im – p – l
imperfect ____________
im – p – f – k
impressed ____________
im – p – s – duh
impressive ____________
im – p – s – v
imprint ____________
im – p – nt
improper ____________
im – p – p – r
improve ____________
im – p – v
improvement ____________
im – p – v – ment

SOUND-SPELLING EXERCISE

c. For words that begin with the letters *imm,* write *im.*

immortal imml
im – m – rt – l
imminent immn
im – m – n – nt

APPLICATION EXERCISE

c. For words that begin with the letters *imm,* write *im.*

immaterial ____________
im – m – t – r – l
immerse ____________
im – m – s
immigrant ____________
im – m – g – nt
immigration ____________
im – m – g – shun
immoderate ____________
im – m – d – r – t
immoral ____________
im – m – r – l

Rule 20	*When you hear the* dis *or* des *sound at the beginning of a word, write a small* d.

SOUND-SPELLING EXERCISE

desolation des – l – shun	dlj	disagree dis – a – g – e	dage
desperate des – p – r – t	dprt	discuss dis – k – s	dks

APPLICATION EXERCISE

desperation des – p – r – shun	________	discount dis – k – nt	________
despise des – p – z	________	discover dis – k – v – r	________
despondent des – p – nd – nt	________	disengage dis – n – g – j	________
despotic des – p – t – k	________	disfavor dis – f – v – r	________
disappoint dis – a – p – oi – nt	________	dismiss dis – m – s	________
discard dis – k – rd	________	disorder dis – o – rd – r	________

Rule 21	*Use the special Stenoscript abbreviations for the salutation and the complimentary closing of a letter.*

a. The salutation

Dear	d	Gentlemen	j
Dear Sir	ds	Dear Mr.	dmr
Dear Madam	dm	Dear Miss	dmi
Dear Ms.	dmz	Dear Mrs.	dms
Ladies and Gentlemen	l&j		

b. The complimentary closing

Cordially	c	Sincerely yours	su
Cordially yours	cu	Yours sincerely	us
Respectfully	r	Yours truly	ut
Very truly yours	vtu	Yours very truly	uvt
Sincerely	s		

These abbreviations are used *only* for the salutation and closing of a letter. For example, the word *sir* is written *sr* except when it is a part of the phrase *Dear Sir.*

WRITING STATE AND CITY NAMES

The United States Postal Service has designated two-letter state abbreviations to be used on envelope addresses. When writing states in your Stenoscript notes, use these same two-letter Postal Service abbreviations. A complete list of United States and Canadian postal abbreviations is presented in the Appendix. Consider the following examples:

Iowa	Ia	Texas	Tx
California	Ca	New York	Ny

City names are written according to the Stenoscript rules. Consider the following examples of how to write city and state names:

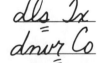

Dallas, Texas	dls Tx	Davenport, Iowa	dvnp/ Ia
Denver, Colorado	dnvr Co	Oakland, California	okl Ca
Green City, Missouri	gn st Mo	Detroit, Michigan	dtyt Mi
Ottawa, Canada	otwa Knda	Atlanta, Georgia	aLa Ga
Springfield, Illinois	spgfd Il	Orlando, Florida	o-o Fl

HIGH-FREQUENCY WORDS: GROUP 3

you your yours	u	over	V	why	y
under	U	we were who whom	w	year	Y
of very	v	week	W	as she was his	3

HIGH-FREQUENCY WORD REVIEW

Write the correct Stenoscript outlines for the following words:

done	________	was	________	know	________
day	________	very	________	under	________
mine	________	and	________	yours	________
the	________	is	________	as	________
nor	________	does	________	of	________
hour	________	so	________	he	________
over	________	him	________		
why	________	all	________		

CONFUSING WORDS

Word	*Definition*
among	use with three or more items
between	use with only two items

She is sitting *among* our invited guests.
The contest is *between* Soraya and Ali.

QUICK COMMA REVIEW

Recalling the punctuation rules from the front of the book, use a comma

e. to set off nouns of direct address.

Dr. Burke, here are the files you requested.
Thank you, Ms. Franklin, for your donation.
That will be all for now, Jim.

f. to set off appositives (nouns or noun phrases that rename or explain a preceding noun or pronoun).

Our salesman, Tom Van Dyke, will demonstrate the Apple IIc.
One of our attorneys, a Notre Dame graduate, will be the speaker.

COMPREHENSIVE WORD REVIEW

Check your progress by writing Stenoscript outlines in your steno pad for the following words:

1. guard
2. our
3. voice
4. she
5. discount
6. century
7. under
8. expert
9. misdirect
10. over
11. why
12. he
13. by
14. on
15. her
16. watch
17. tent
18. ocean
19. function
20. cellar
21. protect
22. mishandling
23. parking
24. inward
25. your
26. hurry
27. who
28. department
29. at
30. am
31. sparkle
32. imprint
33. very
34. his
35. were
36. in
37. feather
38. single
39. pushing
40. wrinkle
41. critic
42. carriage
43. up
44. reporting
45. shorthand
46. of
47. loyal
48. so
49. whom
50. upward
51. as
52. discovery
53. or
54. him
55. impel
56. was
57. saw
58. cement
59. paying
60. position
61. qualify
62. played
63. carry

WRITING EXERCISE

Practice writing these sentences in Stenoscript in your steno pad:

1. We want to thank you for your recent order.
2. It was hard work, and there was no easy way to do it.
3. There were some other papers that I wanted to send with the letter.
4. I am going to work for the Pardon Board.
5. The Personnel Department has a report on the guard.
6. Will you please send us your check for the bill?
7. The regular program on education drew the issue to our attention.
8. The truck traveled in heavy traffic to deliver the cement to the shop.
9. This is a message to tell you that we are pleased with the large order you sent us.
10. If we do not have a reply from you, we will ship the goods tomorrow.

READING, WRITING, AND TRANSCRIPTION EXERCISES

(1)

ds: w wz l dks u
bl w— u. i u l
K l r ofs w K
fnz l — w & s
— rp/ l — blg
dp w— dla.
s

(2)

l & j: w h nlfe u v
r cys f — pzj v
jnrl mngr & w h
h n f r w/ fm
u. // w w— l n
i u sp/ s n —s
mbr z u apvl i
v mp f —s
apy—. uvl

(3)

dm: w r hp l
sa — l r m/ l
dlvr gsy. u k
Kl & u gsy l b
dlvr l u. u zd
n wy — l u o l
b mkl. r dlvy
by i a xp/ n hlg
gsy. // w r s — l
u l nyy uzq —s
svs. vlu

(4)

d bb: — q u f u
nvl l al —
opnq v u pa. d n w
l nyy i. i i K
v u l as s. w l
c u —r. s

(5)

ds: u l w— l h u
Kr n gd rng o f
l K. v w r. y

n ll r xp· lk i
U f u? i K b
pk p l u ofs +
rln l u· —r i
n cf f —s svs·
u l b bl f —
mbrl uz + —r l
b a sml fe f lbr·
K n + c s· ul

(6)

ds: —q u f u
rs— o r· i K n
—s mng + w l
s i O wg dla·
w l lt l gl —
o r —q u w
s l ck o f u·
w l n s —m
l u wg llq u
n· pz ll s n
— nmbr v —z
ilm u l w· i

u w— z m z ih
w k d mc blr
f u· vlu

(7)

dme bnz: w r hp l
rpi l u rs— lbr n
wc u as l b aksp
n r Ks —l kc mn +
wmn bsk skl n
ofs w· u as w—r
r Ks r apv b —
b= v ejk· w r pz
l rpi —l —a h
b apv f Y· 2 Y· aq
w wn a a f —
xl— ppy w gv —
mn + wmn w al— r
Ks // pz s— s a
kp v u b— sifkl +
u dpma· r —r 3
psn w u wd b lq l
h a Q· rq9 u abll?

—s wd hp s
l pss u apkj. //
n a mbr v a fu W.
u l rcv an—r ltr
rg^9 u apkj. l w—
l nkrj u l spk
—l i l b apv &
ll u l pn l b
w— s f — fl
lm. // w l b gd
l A ne f—r
O u ma h. r
nu Kllg l b pbz
nx W. w l s— i
l u —n. ul

(8)

d f: — pps v
—s blln i l nfm
l ryd. o — bk
b= b ma avnu
hrsn blv= sdr avnu
& slm blv= —l a

Kb i b fm f —
ryd. v r bk.
svrl v u nbr h
fl f sm W. —l
—s k— v Kb wd
b v gd f l v s.
w wd pn l gl lg—r
l lk l h Kfe &
dz & l gl blr ag=
w— i an—r. —oz
v s w lrd n i
an—r r egr l bk
ag= w— — nu
ppl w h mv n & l
xcnj ida. f—r —r
r svrl pbm —l —
ryd. v r bk h l
w ll svg. — dm
slmnj l — Knr v
ma & hrsn i i
smpl. i i v s w
l Kl — mr ofs o
z on e Kd n spk

l h z d al_ l
z l z i w w l
Kl z a bk Kb. // w
r s^n _l u l age
w_ s. r bk zd h a
Kb + i i p l —
ryd. l fm 1. l
u al a gl= lg_r
l 6222 hrsn blv=
lmro l 8? w pn
l fnz b 9 0 0. s

(9)

l + j: — jnrl
mnyr v — fm hz
nlfi — b= v drkr
v a nu a/ pn
dvlp b — psnl
dp= . U — lm v
— pn a mpye w
hz pfm — dl v z
jb n a mnr jf l
b e r xl o sprr

b z drkr l b a-
a sm egl l i
W. pa. // ne drkr
w wz l h a vys
n — dfq v a_
l — s pn zd o nfm
— psnl dp=. l
ppzl f a_ . o
mdfk zd b n —
ofs v — psnl drkr
b — — v nx W. //
— b= v drkr i l h
4 W. l dmn — nu
pn + — ppz a_ .
mmbr v — b l
b as l ppz cny i
— a wz. l — — v
4 W. — mlr l b dks
b l — drkr n opn
sj. — dsj v —
drkr l b pbsz —
nx D. i — nu a/
pn i apv b — b

i l b mp— bf
— — v — kr
fskl y. ll n rs—
y — fm hz at a
bns l nu y l
l mpye. — bns
pn l b kp n efk
f — ndfnl fcr
z i i rg- z a
ldj. vlu

(10)

l: — ppzl b ll
fm: jn j wls ll
re: — p9 ll ll
z a mpye w p.
z kr n — p9 ll
r b r fm. f i
mpye. d h a ppzl
—l d —g l g a
lg wa l mpvg—
arng — r. d g
—l ec mpye w i

a—rz l p n r
ll zd h a rzv
p9 spl. — spl wd
b nmbr & — mpye
wd b gvn a lg l
pl o z kr w —
nmbr v z spl o i.
—s wd sv i rkrg
pbm. ll drg — W —r
r m ppl w K l r
ara o sm er— o
o—r. i —z ppl hpn l
b scg f a p9 spl
ar— 8 n — mng
—a f — r ll ml &
n g-. a fu pa n
alnj l — "n p9"
nls & pl n. ll wn
— al— K l 8:30
e f. svrl kr lrd
n — ll. e —n hz
l ck l c w—r —a
blg l mpye. i n

e hz —m lo awa.
H i ec mpyl hz a
rzv & nmbr spl i
wd b ez f — alz
l d a gk ck. e
wd fnz n a fu
mnl & Kd d sm
o-r ls. // I l b
pz. i —s ppzl mrl
u alnz & php i
v — al. f gd
ida. jn j wlo

LESSON 4

Lesson 4 presents Stenoscript Rules 22 through 24, High-Frequency Words Group 4, and appropriate exercises.

Rule 22a	***The long-vowel rule. When the final single consonant sound of a base word is preceded by a long-vowel sound, write the vowel sound but drop the final consonant sound.***

The long-vowel sounds are the *a, e, i, o,* and *u* sounds as they are heard in the following sound-spelling exercises:

SOUND-SPELLING EXERCISE

brake b – a	ba	fine f – i	fi	soon s – u	su
cheap ch – e	ce	home h – o	ho	mute m – u	mu

APPLICATION EXERCISE

alone a – l – o	______	face f – a	______	late l – a	______
aloof a – l – u	______	fake f – a	______	leaf l – e	______
belief b – l – e	______	fame f – a	______	life l – i	______
clean k – e	______	file f – i	______	like l – i	______
deduce d – d – u	______	fire f – i	______	loaf l – o	______
deed d – e	______	hope h – o	______	loose l – u	______
expire x – p – i	______	knife n – i	______	made m – a	______

(continued)

moon ____________
m – u
neat ____________
n – e
niece ____________
n – e
night ____________
n – i
plane ____________
p – a
pole ____________
p – o
price ____________
p – i
rate ____________
r – a
ream ____________
r – e
receipt ____________
r – c – e
remain ____________
r – m – a

ride ____________
r – i
rope ____________
r – o
routine ____________
r – t – e
rude ____________
r – u
rule ____________
r – u
safe ____________
s – a
sale ____________
s – a
scheme ____________
s – k – e
shade ____________
ish – a
shame ____________
ish – a
shape ____________
ish – a

shoot ____________
ish – u
side ____________
s – i
smile ____________
s – m – i
suit ____________
s – u
take ____________
t – a
tape ____________
t – a
time ____________
t – i
train ____________
t – a
tune ____________
t – u
type ____________
t – i
vote ____________
v – o

Rule 22b	*The long-vowel rule is used not only for short words but also for longer words. Just remember to drop the final consonant sound.*

SOUND-SPELLING EXERCISE

educate ejka
e – j – k – a
nominate nmna
n – m – n – a

expedite xpdi
x – p – d – i

APPLICATION EXERCISE

appetite ____________
a – p – t – i
calculate ____________
k – k – l – a

celebrate ____________
s – l – b – a
dominate ____________
d – m – n – a

eliminate e – l – m – n – a	________	parasite p – r – s – i	________
irritate i – r – t – a	________	penetrate p – n – t – a	________
midnight m – d – n – i	________		

Rule 22c	***There is an exception to the long-vowel rule. When the final consonant is a* j, v, *or* z *sound, write those sounds instead of the long-vowel sound.***

SOUND-SPELLING EXERCISE

cage k – j	kj	rose r – z	rz	leave l – v	lv

APPLICATION EXERCISE

achieve a – ch – v	________	freeze f – z	________	rave r – v	________
behave b – h – v	________	fuse f – z	________	receive r – c – v	________
believe b – l – v	________	move m – v	________	save s – v	________
blaze b – z	________	praise p – z	________	tease t – z	________
cave k – v	________	rage r – j	________	wage w – j	________
chose ch – z	________	raise r – z	________	weave w – v	________

APPLICATION EXERCISE

Now try these words. Remember to write the long vowel *unless* it is followed by a *j*, *v*, or *z* sound. Be sure to sound-spell the words as you write them.

brave b – v	________	broke b – o	________	erase e – r – a	________
breeze b z	________	chief ch – e	________	exclude x – k – u	________

(continued)

expose ____________
x – p – z
feel ____________
f – e
froze ____________
f – z
gauge ____________
g – j
hike ____________
h – i
lane ____________
l – a
mail ____________
m – a

nice ____________
n – i
piece ____________
p – e
race ____________
r – a
reduce ____________
r – d – u
relieve ____________
r – l – v
remove ____________
r – m – v
retain ____________
r – t – a

robe ____________
r – o
role ____________
r – o
smoke ____________
s – m – o
trade ____________
t – a
vote ____________
v – o
waive ____________
w – v

Rule 23	*For words ending in the sounds of* ar, er, or, *and* ur, *drop the final* r *and write the vowel sound.*

SOUND-SPELLING EXERCISE

The *ar* sound as pronounced in the following words:

fair fa
f – a
care ka
k – a
wear wa
w – a

The *er* sound as pronounced in the following words:

here he
h – e
cheer ce
ch – e
pier pe
p – e
near ne
n – e

The *or* sound as pronounced in the following words:

roar — ro
r – o

more — mo
m – o

door — do
d – o

pour — po
p – o

The *ur* sound as pronounced in the following words:

sure — zu
ish – u

tour — tu
t – u

pure — pu
p – u

APPLICATION EXERCISE

affair
a – f – a

appear
a – p – e

bare
b – a

bear
b – a

boar
b – o

brochure
b – ish – u

career
k – r – e

chair
ch – a

chore
ch – o

clear
k – e

core
k – o

cure
k – u

dare
d – a

dear
d – e

declare
d – k – a

detour
d – t – u

endure
n – d – u

engineer
n – j – n – e

fare
f – a

fear
f – e

floor
f – o

insure
n – ish – u

(continued)

mature ______
m – t – u/m – ch – u
moor ______
m – u
pear ______
p – a
peer ______
p – e
rare ______
r – a
repair ______
r – p – a
score ______
s – k – o
severe ______
s – v – e
share ______
ish – a

sheer ______
ish – e
sincere ______
s – n – s – e
soar ______
s – o
sore ______
s – o
tier ______
t – e
tore ______
t – o
ware ______
w – a
wear ______
w – a

The following short words are exceptions to this rule:

air	ar	oar	or
ear	er	ore	or

Rule 24	***When you hear the* st *sound, write a capital* S.**

SOUND-SPELLING EXERCISE

estate e – st – a	eSa	sister s – st – r	sSr
stop st – p	Sp	test t – st	tS

APPLICATION EXERCISE

arrest ____________
a – r – st
assist ____________
a – s – st
best ____________
b – st
blast ____________
b – st
capitalist ____________
k – p – t – l – st
cast ____________
k – st
cost ____________
k – st
crust ____________
k – st
destroy ____________
d – st – oi
destruction ____________
d – st – k – shun
detest ____________
d – t – st
enlist ____________
n – l – st
establish ____________
e – st – b – ish
fast ____________
f – st
storage ____________
st – r – j
instrument ____________
n – st – ment
invest ____________
n – v – st
just ____________
j – st
journalist ____________
j – n – l – st
lost ____________
l – st

mast ____________
m – st
mistrust ____________
mis – t – st
most ____________
m – st
novelist ____________
n – v – l – st
persist ____________
p – s – st
protest ____________
p – t – st
register ____________
r – j – st – r
rest ____________
r – st
restrict ____________
r – st – k
rust ____________
r – st
staff ____________
st – f
stand ____________
st – nd
stem ____________
st – m
still ____________
st – l
stock ____________
st – k
twist ____________
t – w – st
vast ____________
v – st
wrist ____________
r – st
youngster ____________
y – ng – st – r

HIGH-FREQUENCY WORDS: GROUP 4

Word(s)	Symbol
about	ao
after	af
again against	ag
any	ne
began begin beginning begun	bg
even ever every	ev
from	fm
off often	of
never	nv
that	-d
their there	-r
these	-z
they	-a
this	-s
those	-oz
upon	pn
where	wa
which	wc
whose	wz
with	w-
without	wo

HIGH-FREQUENCY WORD REVIEW

Write the high-frequency words for the following alphabetic symbols:

z ______
______
______
______

ag ______
______

bg ______
______
______
______

ev ______
______
______

p ______

fm ______

W ______

Y ______

o ______
______
______
______

n ______
______
______
______
______
______
______

r ________ ________ t ________

________ ________ ________

________ ________ ________

CONFUSING WORDS

Word	*Definition*
than	compared to
then	at that time

There are more students in our shorthand class *than* our history class.
I will finish my shorthand homework, and *then* I will have lunch.

QUICK COMMA REVIEW

Remember the following rules for comma usage from the front of the book:

g. Do *not* use a comma to set off closely related appositives.

We secretaries agree with the resolution.

h. Do *not* use a comma to set off one-word appositives.

My sister Irene received her broker's license in 1975.

COMPREHENSIVE WORD REVIEW

Check your progress by writing Stenoscript outlines in your steno pad for the following words:

1. appoint
2. every
3. detachment
4. begin
5. location
6. those
7. diminish
8. upon
9. wrinkled
10. began
11. regular
12. any
13. process
14. there
15. current
16. repair
17. protection
18. again
19. store
20. never
21. still
22. this
23. steer
24. beginning
25. enlistment
26. roar
27. price
28. they
29. remain
30. after
31. educate
32. was
33. save

(continued)

34. you
35. mail
36. carry
37. their
38. sacrifice
39. often
40. receive
41. that
42. engage
43. least
44. feel
45. fell
46. leave
47. very
48. against
49. without
50. nice
51. these
52. undermine
53. extreme
54. hurry
55. remove
56. vote
57. word
58. off
59. exclude
60. with
61. care
62. ever
63. more
64. work
65. order
66. which
67. near
68. from
69. where
70. mistake
71. chore
72. test
73. whose
74. oblige
75. even
76. estate
77. estimate (*n*)
78. begun
79. include
80. destroy
81. forgave

WRITING EXERCISE

Practice writing these sentences in Stenoscript in your steno pad:

1. His fame as a dedicated public servant is widespread.
2. His secretary ordered the roses for the reception.
3. The repairman was ready to stop work when the bell rang for lunch.
4. The assistant to the department head calculated the amount of the bill so that the package could be expedited.
5. The gas tank registered empty, and we still had miles to go before arriving at our destination.
6. It is a shame that there will not be any officers of that group at the formal meeting.
7. The Secretary of State spoke before a meeting of citizens to describe national policy on the war issue.
8. He will make any sacrifice to achieve his goal of fiscal reform.
9. The president of the firm declared that discrimination in hiring had been eliminated.
10. He misjudges his manager when he thinks the work of the parts repair section is being mishandled.

READING, WRITING, AND TRANSCRIPTION EXERCISES

(1)

f: I wd lk l xps
m hi rg f u sl
cy pdk. i i — bS
cy I h ev pcs. —
lS i dfr & pzg.
I h jS o- svrl dzn
pk, l b s— l f.
z ksms gf.// I— l
u wd b pz l he
fm a hp kSmr.
su

(2)

ds: u rgS f a dkpj
v a elklk Splq mze
arv n — mng ma.
w wd lk v mc l
hp u b d n Ry
—s mze. w wd
ppz — l u dks —s
mtr w— sm lg ofs
eqp— fm. —a l b
l ppa l gv u —
dkpj u ne & php.
l arnj f a
dmnSj. uvl

(3)

d my, I m rug l
as u l hp e pn a
lp. dk & I w— l
g l mxko —s fl &
w h m Q. u r —
xp o mxko o w— l
u me h sm ida.
zd w g b la o b
ar? la lvl i mo
rlx. w wd h lk l
nzy — l ska & ma
f. o — o r h
mag — lp b ar

wd b mc fSr + wd
gv s mo li n mxko.
wl d u — g? // af w
arv n mxko w xpk
l r — a kr. php
u wd hp s w —
ida v pa l vzl.
d u h — na v sm
gd hll? w — ll v
almsfe v ks! // lS
b n lS my w ne
l ke — kS v — a
lp l a mnmn.
ne h. f svg mne
l b mS lk. // m
— g. f u hp. gv r
rg. l lm + —
cdn. s

(4)

ds: r akq ofs hz
pS f- l s a Sa
zoq — l u ak i

pS d. ak9 l r
rk. u h n ma —
lS 2 pa. o u lo. //
r kdl plc i lbrl + w
— g — lm u r age
w — u r fa. H i u
lk kz l ma u pa
z Spla w r lg l dks
nu lm. php a dny
v u lo wd b no. //
pz Sp n o ru + ll s
n — lm ll wc u
kd bq l rpa —
am — u o. u l
f — l r kdl ofsr
r USq + rd l hp
n wlev wa — a k.
ma w xpk l he
fm u su? vlu

(5)

dms jnz: w r sy
l nlfe u — l — dz

u o r O v Sk.
ma w ppz an r ne
pln? i i Kl ev go
& i hz b v pplr
w m v r dkmnag
KSmr. u l f pkcr
v s pln & a dkpj
v l — pe n —
nkz ilSa Kllg. i
K n bu pg & lo r.
— lS pi i — sa
z — pi v — pln
u o. H drg r
fl sa w K ofr
u a 10 ps
dk. ll w r zu u
l n b dapy w
ev go. w l b pz
l pss u o z su
z i rc r ofs. ma
w he fm u b rln
ma? uvl

(6)

i u li a rfzg dg
u l w l li nu
b sf dg. nu b
i a nu kbna dg
ma fm — fiS dSl
wbr n — KeS mS
mdn bllg p n —
wd. u l lS re
fu for n nu b.
nu b lS blr bkz
i i blr. b nu b
— nx li u g zpg.
u hzb & u cdn l
g u & u f. l
g u r a pfk
hSs.

(7)

d de admz: g u
v mc f — ne vzl
I h w u — or
D. i z w sm

hzlz —l I dsi n
l ma fml apkj f
— vknc z rjSr v
— jnr klj, wr l
l a fi pzj I d n
fe —l I wz l ma
a rdkl cnj l —s li.//
I z v mc mps b
l u ld e v — nu
klj s—r & u pn f
fcr xpnj, l l h fnq
l —q —l sc a
fi vncr l b llan
n a nbrhd —l ne
l O mc, l l n lk
v rspk f wl u r
d n —l nbrhd —l
ma e fe —l I m
n — ri psn f —
jb l —s li.// I wz
u — gaS skss n
l u pn f — klj,
I fe zu —l l l lrd
mag a ga sklSk
mpj n — ara, swrl
v m yq hi sku
f. h lrd dsi l
ma apkj f nro—!
uvl

(8)

l: Sf v — nu pgm//
fm: dp— hd//
re: nu pn// w arv
l — flog pvyl dsj
drq r meq lS W://
1+—r l a re ne f
a pgm v —s li.// 2+
l l la a lq li l
dvlp.// 3+ Sf mmbr
l h l dvo mS v
—r li l l alo.// 4+
—r mS b a s—r
wa mmbr k gl lg—r
l w ll sl drkj.//
5+ a age o — bsk

asmpj v — pgm l h
l b arv l wn a
fu D v bq — w. //
6) smpl mtrl mS b
ppa b nx fl. // 7)
w zd la a ko lk
l — pgm wn w
r n a pzj l ma
sm dla ppzl. // bf
lS w lll pgs h b
ma. — s i bkz w
h l b nvv n s
o-r pjk — l la a
gd de v li. i i
—rf uj — l w b
rle fm o-r dl l
sp l r li o — s
mp— pjk. // I m
asq — l — drkr la
akj l c l i — l w
r l fe fm o-r
okpj l w o — s
pjk alo. I m zu

— l — s k b arnj
& — l w l b pml
l S w su. bl
pr

(9)

l: dp— hd // fm:
a mpye // re: a
ppzl // I wd li l
ppz a wa v h lq —
laq v a nu mpye
n r dp—. I wd li
l ppz — l ec nu
mpye b zon l —
m dfr k. v w
— l r d he. I fr
ppz — l e b ll —
— q aq pcjr — l r
mp— l m & l — oz
w mS w w — m
— q — l me la y l
li o-rjz. // l ilSa
ll e uz a mr ≠ z

a nu mpye + msf
z z gi-// a fu D. bf
mr x arv. l la V
z jb — hd v —
dp ll. — Sf — l
a nu mpye i
arvg + — l jn jnz
i l b z gi- ec
psn n — dp wd
b nvr l f sm
pe v w — l mi
b asi l mr x-//
af z arvl mr jnz
wd c l i — l mr
x. li — fS fu D.
wd b sp o —
vyg asi. ppz b
— Sf- mr x wd
—s me — Sf n
sml gu w a lll
o ec v — pyk.
— l r ll wa vzl—
lby + ln ag wl w

h d n — pS-//
—s pn wd am—
l llg lor=lvl mpye.
hl — lag prd-
— bnft v d i —s
wa r m:// 1+ hi=
rgg mpye r of l bz
l V z dla-//2+
a nu mpye wd apc
lor=lvl mpye w—
gar ez-// 3+ —
nu mpye i bon
n b sm/ w
i l ag— w—
w e mS ln l d-//
I l b hp l q nl
gar dla ag —s
ppzl i mnz— o
wz- Km bkr

LESSON 5

Lesson 5 presents Stenoscript Rule 25 on brief forms, Stenoscript outlines for contractions, and appropriate exercises.

Rule 25	*Memorize the 30 Stenoscript brief forms. Study and practice the brief forms until you can write them quickly and accurately.*

accompany	ac	business	bz	organize	og
accomplish	ac	company	co	particular	prt
acknowledge	ak	corporate	crp	recommend	rec
administer	adm	government	gvt	represent	rp
advantage	avj	immediate	imd	responsible	rsp
advertise	adv	individual	ndv	satisfy	st
anticipate	ant	information	nfo	situation	sit
appreciate	ap	manufacture	mf	specify	spc
approximate	apx	merchandise	mds	suggestion	sug
associate	as	opportunity	op	supervise	spv

Use the brief form for all related forms of the word it represents. For example, the related forms of *acknowledge* would be written as follows:

acknowledge	ak	acknowledgment	ak
acknowledged	ak	acknowledges	aḳ
acknowledging	ak¯		

Thus the related forms of *organize* would be written *og*. The context of the sentence will tell you which form to use.

organize	og	organizational	og
organized	og_	organizing	og
organizer	og	organizable	og
organization	og	organizes	og.

To avoid misinterpretations in reading and transcribing, use the dot to indicate plurals or the third-person singular form of verbs, as in *organizes*. Use the underline to indicate past tense, as in *organized*.

APPLICATION EXERCISE

association	________	administration	________
corporation	________	accompanied	________
immediate	________	corporative	________
manufacturer	________	individual	________
situation	________	particularly	________
governmental	________	responsible	________
accomplish	________	advertise	________
company	________	advantage	________
individually	________	supervisory	________
opportunity	________	approximate	________
administrative	________	organization	________
approximately	________	information	________
particular	________	merchandise	________
representative	________	appreciation	________

manufactured	________	informational	________
representing	________	representation	________
satisfactory	________	specify	________
immediately	________	associate	________
merchandising	________	specific	________
satisfaction	________	recommendation	________
responsibility	________	anticipation	________
specification	________	suggested	________
accomplishing	________	opportunities	________

HIGH-FREQUENCY WORD REVIEW

All the high-frequency words that you memorized in Lessons 1 through 4 are listed on this and the following page for reference and review.

a an	a
and	&
be been being by bye buy but	b
see seen seeing	c
says	sz
do due did done doing	d
does	dz
day	D
he me	e
for	f
go gone going	g
goes	gz
had have having	h
I	I
saw us	s
if it is its	i

(continued)

can, come, came, coming	k
all, well, will	l
mine, my, am, him, many	m
month	M
in, neither, know, no, none, nor, not	n
or, on, owe, so	o
out	O
up	p
are, her, hers, our, ours, hour	r
even, ever, every	ev
has	hz
at, to, too	t
the	—
you, your, yours	u
under	U
of, very	v
over	V
we, were, who, whom	w
week	W
why	y
year	Y
as, she, was, his	z
about	aO
after	af
again, against	ag
any	ne
from	fm
however	H
off, often	of
never	nv
question	Q
that	—t
their, there	—r
these	—z
they	—a
this	—s
those	—oz
upon	pn
where	wa
which	wc
whose	wz
with	w—
without	w—O
began, begin, beginning, begun	bg

CONTRACTIONS

Contractions are formed using the standard Stenoscript rules. To avoid confusion, however, use an apostrophe above the word to indicate a contraction. Practice the following contractions until you can write them quickly and accurately:

can't	K'	hasn't	hz'	won't	w'
couldn't	Kd'	I'll	I'l	wouldn't	wd'
doesn't	dz'	shouldn't	zd'	you'll	u'l
don't	d'	we're	w'r		

CONFUSING WORDS

Word	*Definition*
its	possessive
it's	it is

That computer and *its* many software packages can be purchased.
It's a perfect interview suit!

QUICK COMMA REVIEW

Recalling the punctuation rules from the front of the book, use a comma

i. to set off a direct quotation.

"What time is the meeting," Bob asked, "and where will it be?"

j. to separate two or more adjectives that modify the same noun when the word *and* is appropriate but omitted.

Please use the enclosed, stamped envelope for your reply.

Note: Do *not* use a comma when the first adjective modifies the second adjective.

Sarah noted several glaring grammatical errors in the manuscript.

Note: Use a hyphen for compound adjectives when they precede a noun they modify. Do *not* use a hyphen when the compound adjectives follow the noun.

The well-known speaker received a standing ovation.
The speaker was well known.

COMPREHENSIVE WORD REVIEW

Check your progress by writing Stenoscript outlines in your steno pad for the following words:

1. situation
2. done
3. for
4. a
5. the
6. in
7. go
8. mine
9. an
10. year
11. too
12. no
13. gone
14. him
15. and
16. he
17. know
18. to
19. going
20. many
21. be
22. accomplish
23. you
24. she
25. after
26. never
27. upon
28. which
29. whose
30. his
31. week
32. again
33. any
34. by
35. see
36. am
37. my
38. owe
39. not
40. as
41. we
42. they
43. begin
44. with
45. month
46. had
47. nor
48. saw
49. her
50. up
51. at
52. under
53. of
54. against
55. this
56. that
57. over
58. who
59. why
60. was
61. those
62. did
63. it
64. day
65. so
66. neither
67. goes
68. being
69. began
70. ever
71. often
72. these
73. very
74. yours
75. begun
76. been
77. having
78. if
79. will
80. are
81. or
82. none
83. all
84. can
85. have
86. seen
87. due
88. off
89. there
90. appreciate
91. from
92. were
93. business
94. buy
95. every
96. individual
97. even
98. whom
99. opportunity
100. out
101. about
102. do
103. represent
104. on
105. come
106. satisfy
107. corporation
108. immediately

WRITING EXERCISE

In your steno pad, practice writing these sentences and paragraphs in Stenoscript:

A. Sentences

1. The national organization will handle all hotel reservations, but each individual is responsible for making his own travel arrangements.
2. If you are not satisfied with the merchandise, the company will refund your money.
3. An individual should be appointed who would be responsible for administering the self-education program.
4. These meetings provide an excellent opportunity for managers of small businesses to exchange information about similar problems.
5. There are approximately ten manufacturers who could make this product according to our specifications.
6. Every questionnaire should be accompanied by a form letter explaining the purpose of this study.
7. We must find a solution to the present situation immediately.
8. Each company has been asked to send at least one representative to the meeting on business-government relations.
9. We were particularly pleased to learn that you do appreciate the difficulty of the situation.
10. Who is responsible for obtaining detailed information about the corporate structure of the company?

B. Paragraphs

Some pairs of words that express opposite meanings are the following: over and under, in and out, before and after, for and against, this and that, these and those, many and few, every and none, particular and general, begin and end, come and go, buy and sell, acknowledge and ignore, either and neither, or and nor, ever and never, business and pleasure.

On the other hand, some pairs of words that express similar meanings are the following: accomplish and do, manufacture and make, pleased and satisfied, immediate and present, approximate and near, appreciate and thank, personal and individual, merchandise and goods, association and company.

READING, WRITING, AND TRANSCRIPTION EXERCISES

(1)

dmr ra: w lk —s
op l asS — gvl
n png — njwr
Sd v vkgl rhbly.
wr — ls i a
enms l w fe —l
w— gd og i k b
ac wn — li all
& w— a mnmm
am— v dfkl. // w
wd —rf li l me
w— — rp. fm u
dp— —s W o —l
w ma bq png imd.
s

(2)

dmr jnsn: — ac
bzu l gv u — nfo
—l u rqS ag—
dvlp— smnr f
psnl adm mngr.
z u l c — smnr
hz b og n 2 p: l
sl — prl ne v ndv.
n m sil. // — fS
p Kor — plc rsp.
v — psnl ofsr gv.
nfo —l l hp m
US— wl plc i —
wa i i ma & adm &
wl — ke psnl izu r
lg. // — sk p v
— smnr dks. —
ro v — psnl ofsr
& z rlyp w— mngr.
i de w— sc lpk z
— ncr v Sf pzj.
hw l dlmn —
S. f Sf psnl
ofsr & hw l mpv

ndv ac n Sf pzj.
— u blr dlgj og +
mny— v le-// i u
wz l plspa n —s
smnr w sug —l u
api imd bkz rzSj
i lml l 15 ndv.
vlu

(3)

dmr jnz: z u rgS
bb sm— r co rp
n u dSk l b klg
o u nx W l dks
u mds pbm // mr
sm— hz b as w
r mf co f m Y. +
i fmbr w —
opry v a sml bz-
e l sp — afnu
w — u dksg —
pbm v u prl bz

n — ho v Kag
a mo sl sa sul
f u- vlu

(4)

l: mpye l — Ny
hdq! // fm: — pzd //
re: — apy— v jn
jnz // i i a pzr l
nlfi u —l mr jn jnz
hz b apy— dla= pssg
mnyr v r Ny hdq!-
mr jnz l pz —
rynl mnyr v —
plsbg opry jyn —
fm n 1984 + z
apy- asS rynl
mnyr n q v dla
pssg l plsbg —
flog Y.// mr jnz
bg l z nu pzj
a dlnsv bkg n
elklnx. + dla pssg z

l z bd nly v r
fm. U z drky w
xpk l mpv r
opry he l — Ny
hdq:. e l b n q
v svsq nu ak: n
— Ny ara. e hz
lo b as l sc f
wa l mpv — fo
v rp: fm hdq:
l — rynl ofs. //
mr jnz pn l bq
mrs jnz & —r 3
cdn l mnhln l
lv. // w w l lk
jn jnz l r hdq:
& as u l hp m
n z nu pzj. rnd
bc

(5)

dmr jnsn: I zd li
l ak u rs— llr

n wc u ma apky
f a pzj z a pgmr
w— — co. u
glfky f — jb r
mpsv nde. // w r
a sml crp —l v mc
ne l xp— i dla=
pssg opry. lS m
w w a— a mpt
gvl jb —l l nly r
bz a ga de. b w
r l awa —l —fo
v dla n sm v r
opry i l pz— so &
nefz—. // w l h l
apx lpl r spe n
svrl ara i w r l
Ke l — lm v r
age— w— — gvl. //
w wd li l la Sp.
l hi u imd. H u
mS US— —l i la
li l dvlp & og nu

dla psag opry. ma
w gl n lc w— u
n ag 3 M? I no
—l u r mpy l
pz. I ho —rf
—l —s dla l n
pv u fm png l
jyn s l a lar da
pvg v ks —l u
apky i apv b r
psnl, dp. // w r
lkg f l heg fm
u ag su. vsu

(6)

dmr mly: i i w
mx feg —l I ru
u lD ag a mpt
cny n r og. f 8
y mr wlm aln hz
ip r og n u ipn.
w h rcv V — y
m lbr fm l v u

n pz v mr aln.
w. w l h b v
pz w z w z
r rp n — fd. //
mr aln aksp lS
W wl i f m a
sgnfk pmy. —
pyd v r co hz
jS apy m vr=pyd
n cy v KSmr rly.
n —s nu pz l
l spv — f. v
l r rp —ug —
Knly. e l —rf Sl
b nvv w u fm
lo n a mo rmo
pz. // mr aln. lS
vzl l u co l la pa
smle nx M o u l h
a op l c m ag bf
e la p z nu dl.
w n u l jyn
w s n wzg m

l n z nu pz . //
mr tms lv i tag
V mr aln. dl & l
ac m o z nx lp
n — fd . w fe
s — l u l b pz
w — mr lv. w &
— u l f m l
b a v pz &
tl yg mn . ul

(7)

dmi ga: u as — l
d s — u a rp v
m lp l H . z d
US i u luS as
wd li l bK awa v
— mrl v & fa n
— og & png fcr v
— s lu & n — svs
ofr b hll rSr &
arli . // d m hp l
rp — l n jnrl —q.

w — l . php. u
wd li e l Kvr
sm dla . // —
arli arnj . w sm
& d z n rgi l
pa f Vwa lgj . u l
rmmbr — l d z
smwl aphnsv o — l
sko . // o — mng
af arvl — mmbr v
— lu gu ml l —
hll w — mr fnl r
gi . e ge s l pz —
14 psn n — gu l
l an — r & gv s
Kp v — dla dnry .
—n e dlvr a f lkcr
o H & o — pa w
w l vzl . e z a
rsp & nlly rp v
u as . — gu z
pz — l e z l ac
s . // — hll f —

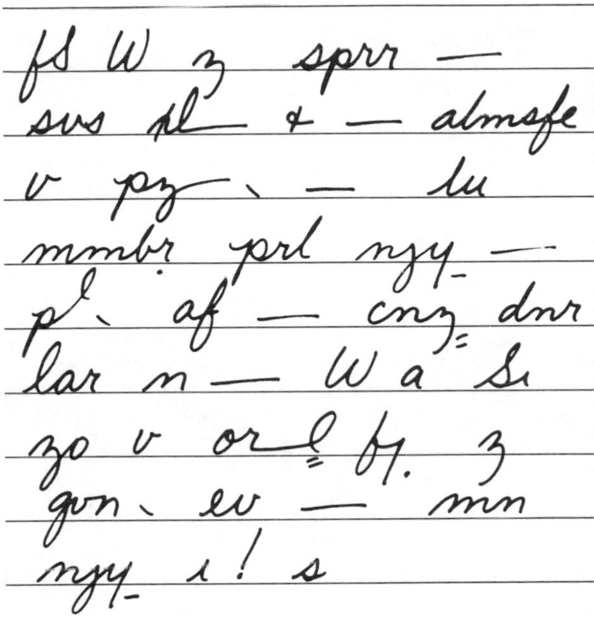

(8)

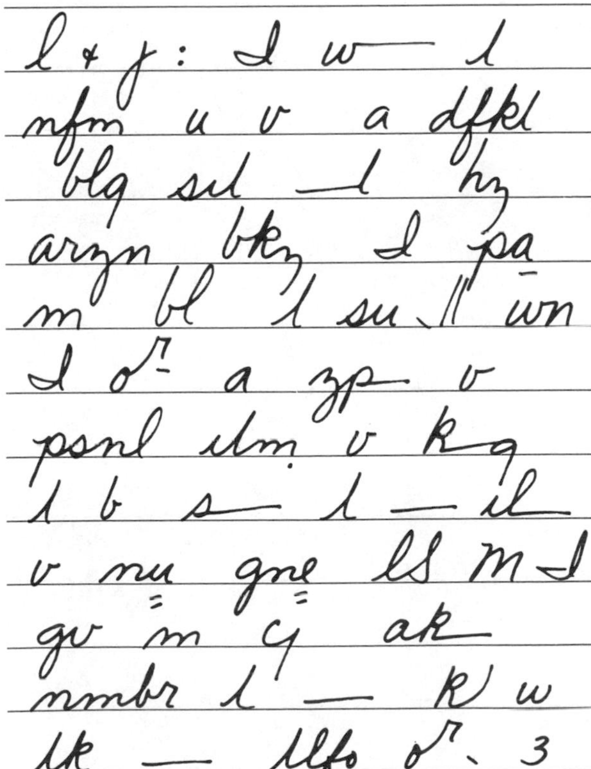

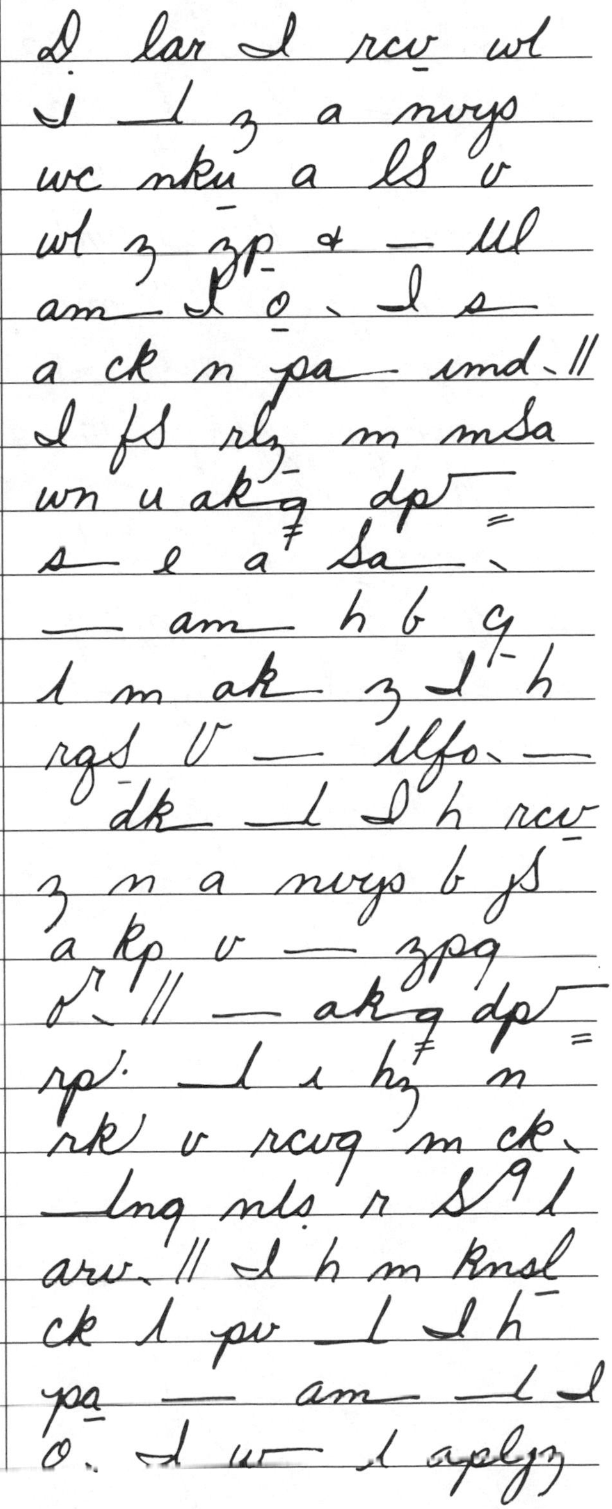

f m err & l — sa
le py O — l u co
mS h sm rk v
m pa — . ll I wd
ap ne f u K ma
l rzv — s sil . I
m nkzq flkp. v
m rs — bl & v
m Knsl ck . I h
n Kp v — zpq
Sa — . I nkz — l
Sa — w — m ck
wn I ma pa — .
ul

LESSON 6

Lesson 6 presents Stenoscript Rules 26 through 30 and appropriate exercises.

Rule 26	*When you hear the* com, con, contra, *or* counter *sound at the beginning of a word, write a small* k.

SOUND-SPELLING EXERCISE

commerce kms
  com – m – s
compact kpk
  com – p – k
confirm kfm
  con – f – m
connect knk
  con – n – k
contract ktk
  con – t – k
counteract kak
  counter – a – k

APPLICATION EXERCISE

combat ______
  com – b – t
commission ______
  com – m – shun
compass ______
  com – p – s
compel ______
  com – p – l
compete ______
  com – p – e
concern ______
  con – s – n
condemn ______
  con – d – m
connection ______
  con – n – k – shun
consent ______
  con – s – nt
constant ______
  con – st – nt
contradict ______
  contra – d – k
control ______
  con – t – o
counterattack ______
  counter – a – t – k
counterfeit ______
  counter – f – t
counterpart ______
  counter – p – rt

Rule 27	*When you hear the* enter, inter, intra, *or* intro *sound at the beginning of a word, write a capital* N.

SOUND-SPELLING EXERCISE

enter enter	N	intramural intra – m – r – l	Nmrl
interfere inter – f – e	Nfe	introduction intro – d – k – shun	Ndkj

APPLICATION EXERCISE

entering enter – ng	________	intermix inter – m – x	________
enterprise enter – p – z	________	international inter – n – shun – l	________
intercept inter – s – p	________	interval inter – v – l	________
interim inter – m	________	interview inter – v – u	________
interject inter – j – k	________	interworking inter – w – rk – ng	________
intermediate inter – m – d – t	________	introductory intro – d – k – t – ree	________

Rule 28a	*When you hear the* ble *(pronounced* bul*) sound at the end of a word, write a capital* B.

SOUND-SPELLING EXERCISE

able a – bul	aB	libel l – bul	lB
symbol s – m – bul	smB	possible p – s – bul	psB

APPLICATION EXERCISE

Bible ____________
b – bul
cable ____________
k – bul
disable ____________
dis – a – bul
double ____________
d – bul
enable ____________
n – a – bul
feeble ____________
f – bul
impossible ____________
im – p – s – bul

incapable ____________
n – k – p – bul
label ____________
l – bul
legible ____________
l – j – bul
rebel ____________
r – bul
stable ____________
st – bul
trouble ____________
t – bul

Rule 28b	***When adding the* ble *(pronounced* bul*) sound to a base word, just add a capital* B.**

SOUND-SPELLING EXERCISE

Base Word

agree age
a – g – e
desire dzi
d – z – i
vary vy
v – ree

Addition of ble *(*bul*) sound*

agreeable ageB
a – g – e – bul
desirable dziB
d – z – i – bul
variable vyB
v – ree – bul

APPLICATION EXERCISE

deniable ____________
d – n – i – bul
disagreeable ____________
dis – a – g – e – bul

identifiable ____________
i – d – nt – f – i – bul
justifiable ____________
j – st – f – i – bul

(continued)

peaceable ______
p – e – bul

reliable ______
r – l – i – bul

suitable ______
s – u – bul

verifiable ______
v – r – f – i – bul

Rule 29a	*Use a comma to represent the* nce *or* nse *(pronounced* ence*) sound at the end of a word. To avoid confusion with the comma used for punctuation, this comma is always attached to the preceding letter.*

SOUND-SPELLING EXERCISE

chance 
ch – nce

dense 
d – nse

since 
s – nce

Note: Begin the upstroke of the preceding letter before writing the comma.

APPLICATION EXERCISE

absence ______
a – b – s – nce

balance ______
b – l – nce

dance ______
d – nce

enhance ______
n – h – nce

evidence ______
e – v – d – nce

excellence ______
x – l – nce

expense ______
x – p – nse

fence ______
f – nce

finance ______
f – n – nce

ignorance ______
i – g – n – r – nce

influence ______
n – f – nce

intense ______
n – t – nse

once ______
w – nce

patience ______
p – ish – nce

reference ______
r – f – r – nce

rinse ______
r – nse

sense ______
s – nse

tense ______
t – nse

Rule 29b	*When the* nce *or* nse *(pronounced* ence*) sound occurs in the middle of a word, write* ns *for the* ence *sound.*

If the comma were used to represent the *nce* sound in the middle of a word, it would be difficult to write and transcribe. Therefore, the comma should be used for the *ence* sound only at the end of a word.

SOUND-SPELLING EXERCISE

Base Word

dance
d – nce

intense
n – t – nse

Written Out

dancing
d – n – s – ng
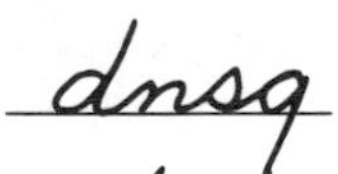

intensive
n – t – n – s – v

Rule 29c	*When adding* nce *or* nse *(pronounced* ence*) to a base word, just add a comma.*

SOUND-SPELLING EXERCISE

Base Word

appear
a – p – e
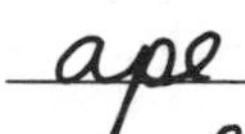

resist
r – z – st

Written Out

appearance
a – p – e – nce

resistance
r – z – st – nce
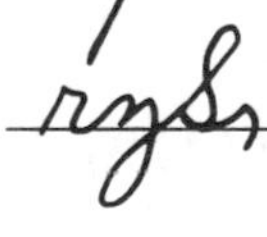

APPLICATION EXERCISE

annoyance ____________
a – n – oi – nce

appliance ____________
a – p – i – nce

clearance ____________
k – e – nce

defiance ____________
d – f – i – nce

reliance ____________
r – l – i – nce

variance ____________
v – ree – nce

Rule 30	*When you hear the* eeus, shul, *or* shus *sound, write a small* x.

SOUND-SPELLING EXERCISE

a. The *eeus* sound

courteous kx
k – rt – eeus

nucleus nkx
n – k – eeus

devious dvx
d – v – eeus

APPLICATION EXERCISE

curious ____________
k – r – eeus

dubious ____________
d – b – eeus

envious ____________
n – v – eeus

glorious ____________
g – r – eeus

hideous ____________
h – d – eeus

mysterious ____________
mys – t – r – eeus

obvious ____________
o – b – v – eeus

previous ____________
p – v – eeus

serious ____________
s – r – eeus

tedious ____________
t – d – eeus

various ____________
v – r – eeus

victorious ____________
v – k – t – r – eeus

SOUND-SPELLING EXERCISE

b. The *shul* sound

facial fx
f – shul

official ofx
o – f – shul

partial px
p – shul

residential rzdnx
r – z – d – n – shul

APPLICATION EXERCISE

beneficial ____________
b – n – f – shul

credential ____________
k – d – n – shul

crucial ____________
k – shul

essential ____________
e – s – n – shul

financial ____________
f – n – n – shul

influential ____________
n – f – n – shul

judicial ____________
j – d – shul

potential ____________
p – t – n – shul

racial ____________
r – shul

social ____________
s – shul

special ____________
s – p – shul

superficial ____________
s – p – f – shul

SOUND-SPELLING EXERCISE

c. The *shus* sound

anxious 
a – nk – shus

spacious 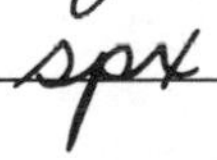
s – p – shus

conscientious 
con – she – n – shus

APPLICATION EXERCISE

ambitious ____________
a – m – b – shus

atrocious ____________
a – t – shus

delicious ____________
d – l – shus

ferocious ____________
f – r – shus

fictitious ____________
f – k – t – shus

gracious ____________
g – shus

judicious ____________
j – d – shus

malicious ____________
m – l – shus

pretentious ____________
p – t – n – shus

repetitious ____________
r – p – t – shus

suspicious ____________
s – s – p – shus

vicious ____________
v – shus

HIGH-FREQUENCY WORD REVIEW

Write the correct Stenoscript outlines for the following words:

about	________	the	________	she	________
began	________	whom	________	over	________
beginning	________	where	________	does	________
any	________	however	________	its	________
those	________	question	________	and	________
up	________	again	________	him	________
owe	________	even	________	neither	________
under	________	begun	________	who	________
has	________	ever	________	which	________
goes	________	upon	________	answer	________
see	________	so	________	on	________
he	________				

CONFUSING WORDS

Word	*Definition*
except	but
accept	receive

Everyone *except* Mary came to school today.
Please *accept* this small gift as a token of my appreciation.

Word	*Definition*
affect (*verb*)	influence
effect (*noun*)	result

Rising interest rates will *affect* the stock market.
The *effect* of rising interest rates is not yet known.

QUICK COMMA REVIEW

Recalling the punctuation rules from the front of the book, use a comma

k. before and after the day, date, and year. Do *not* use a comma when the date is expressed without the year or when the month and year are expressed without the date.

  Our attorney will be here on Wednesday, August 10, 1990, to brief us.
  The dedication of the new Byers Building will be November 2 at 2 p.m.
  Plans for acquiring the property should be completed by May 1990.

l. to separate the elements within an address and to separate the city and the state. Do *not* use a comma to separate the state and zip code.

  Please mail the package to Sue Williams, 702 Maple Road, Chicago, IL 60612, after September 5.

  They plan to visit Detroit, Michigan, later this summer.

COMPREHENSIVE WORD REVIEW

Check your progress by writing Stenoscript outlines in your steno pad for the following words:

1. tense
2. balance
3. concern
4. appear
5. introduce
6. various
7. entered
8. essential
9. double
10. raise
11. commerce
12. after
13. staff
14. convention
15. suitable
16. legible
17. obvious
18. ambitious
19. proceed
20. commission
21. approximately
22. suspicious
23. dubious
24. chance
25. commercial
26. responsibility
27. instrument
28. capable
29. clearance
30. where
31. even
32. impossible
33. since
34. influence
35. interviewed
36. sentences
37. serious
38. connected
39. chose
40. individuality
41. late
42. blast
43. label
44. social
45. reference
46. crucial
47. whose
48. beginning
49. corporation
50. entertain
51. continue
52. expanse
53. hideous
54. financial

(continued)

55. their
56. achieve
57. against
58. counterfeit
59. appreciation
60. ever
61. satisfied
62. specification
63. establish
64. spacious
65. any
66. contradict
67. often
68. upon
69. manufacturing
70. never
71. again
72. mistrust

WRITING EXERCISE

Practice writing these sentences in Stenoscript in your steno pad:

1. The controversy is liable to continue for some time.
2. The consent of city officials is essential to the success of our enterprise.
3. For reasons of national security, it is essential that the identity of our informant be concealed.
4. Our organization tries to provide every capable individual with the opportunity to assume a position of responsibility.
5. The evidence indicates that the majority of people are concerned because of the current international situation.
6. No facilities suitable for our purpose are available in this city.
7. The company representative assured us that his organization manufactures appliances of the very finest quality.
8. A special organization has been formed to improve social conditions in our community.
9. We are confident that the social welfare plans will be approved by the special presidential commission.
10. It is difficult but possible to control all of the variable factors in order to remedy the present situation.

READING, WRITING, AND TRANSCRIPTION EXERCISES

(1)

dm: w wd b pz-
l h u as uz r
fslt f u meq. w
h spx ra f nnpfl
og & w wd ma ev
f l la Ka v u
prl ne. // I m s^n
—l suB arnj kb
ma & I wd b hp
l me w— u l u
Ronj l dks —s
mlr f r. su

(2)

j: f vrx rzn w
r Ksdrg mvg r
nk bz og l u
sl. // r mf p—
wd b a spx l
& wd rqi a KsdrB
am— v l. s, w
r prl NS n fslt
f efz— zpq v r
mds w wd ap nfo
Ksng pp^l f sa n
— imd vsnl v—
raro y. // ne hp —l
u K gv s l b mS
lk. ul

(3)

dmr K^r: w h a lb
fm ms Krl mgn
apiq f a adm pzj
w— r og. w wd
li l vrfi — da v
r al, l u sku
& l rcv a rk v
r ga. // ne nfo rg^a
r Krkbr & dpbll l
lo b ap. s, z wd

b d sm v Kfdnx
w i i esnx —l
w ln l —l w K v
r bkg, ne sc
nfo l b hd n Sk
Kfds, // a Sm
ads nvlo i nkz
f u Kons n rpig,
—g u f u asSs n
—s mtr, ul

(4)

ds: l zo r ap f
u pmp pa— f —
apis u pcs a z/
li aq w h gvn u
a spx dk—, i hz
b Kdl l u ak— z
zon b — spx nle
o — nkz Sa—, //
w ho —l u l nyy
— hi = gll mds u
h pcs + w lk f

l svq u n — fcr,
s

(5)

ds: w r pz l ln
—l u r NS n rp
r co n deq w —
gvl, z u n w h b
n — mf bz f apx
a sncy, drg —l li
w h h v sl bz rlq
w — — vrx crp +
gvl ajnc w h dl
w—, w fe —l r
skss i d l — hi
Klbr v r psnl z
l z l — hi gll
v r mds, // w wd
—rf ap u sq s
a Kpe rK v u
pS mpy + ne
o r nfo —l u fe
ma hp s n maq

r dsj. sj —
prl jb f wc u r
apig K le l —
pzj v sa mnjr w
r lkq f a kpt
rlB ndv w — adm
abll z l z mds
xprs. // i u zd h
ne O. Ksng u
apkj d n hzla l
klk s. s

jj & — l u r ne
n evq u d. a
pz — smi & vyp l
hp l Kvj r v u
abll l gl alq w
ppl prl w — flo
mpye. // rmmbr l
h akrl & Kpe nfo
Ksng — na & ads
v ndv w r glfi &
lq l gv u a rfrs.

(6)

wn u r b Nvu f
a jb i i mp
— l — fS mpj —
mpyr hz v u i a
gd l. // u apes
& psnll l nfs r
opnn v u. u zd
b ds n sc a wa
— l — Nvur l fe
— l u h gd lS &

(7)

d mr sm—: I h b
lrq l rc u b fo sj
lS W b h lB fgu
n. l v — nssybdq
mbrl f u nu gjr
avaB. i i v ga mp
— l w skjl a Kfrs
z su z psB. —
meg K b arnj l u
Kvnj. I l n l

pbbll b n — vsnl
v u ho lmS ev
D f — rS v —s
W. i wd b n 1B
l l f e l c u l
lmS ne li. ll —r
r svrl —g. I w—
l dks w— u.
fS i i esnx —l
w spl O — dla.
v r Klk. I m lo
agx l Kpe —
fnnx arny. . w
Kn Kms i —z
Klk r n Kpe.
— Ksgs v fr
dla Kd b srx. i i
psB f nSs —l r
w^mn l su b bz
o an—r Klk. a
dla v ev a fu D.
K smli ma gi a
bg dfrs. —r i lwz

— cs v bd w—r.
b mag fnl arny.
su w K avyd ne
nkons + sps —l me
o—rwz rzl. ws —
mlr. I mny r sll
I m Kfd —l —g.
l mv ri alg. I n
u l ap — wzdm
v Kzg r de bf —
— v — W. ll ws
ag ll e azu u —l
r w l b v — hS
gll. w h h z u n
a gd bl v sprs w
jb. sc z u. — Kpls
v r Kznx w^mn +
—r Kpsl f fS w
i v l nn. — sprul
v r mtrl i lo a
mlr v rk. ll I
l li l Klk u b
fo smli n — nx

fu D. ı ı ı ageB
w K —n arnj l me
& lk —q V. vlu

(8)

dm: —s llr ı n
rsp, l u rs—
rgS f nfo. r co hz
h a ga de v sprj
w— fnnx pbm v
— k— u dki. n
r Kpsl z lgl & fnnx
Ksl. w de w— m
Kpx mbr. u K h
Kpe Kfd, n r abll
l hl ne evncll.//
w —q ı dzıB l me
w— r K. n psn
wnev psB. s, u
lv n — vsnl d
wd li l sug —l
w pn a Kfrs. w
R me l — co. ma

ofs l u Kvns. ı
ı dzıB —l u ll
s n a D ahd l
— laS. —n e r
d o m as K arnj
l b avaB.// l r Kfrs
w l h a c, l dks
ne mbr v mp l u.
w K ksdr u lbll
nzus — bl, v pa.
o u mgj & —kpnsj
d u fm — co wa
u w mpy. —z &
ne o—r mbr v Ksn
l rcv r pmp &
K^x alnj. ı ı ı
psB pz b zu l bq
w— u l r Kfrs l
— rlv rk. llr &
o—r ppr u ma h—
—a l klbu l r
fmlrl w— u sil.//
w, u dsı pn a da

f r Kfrs pz Klk
— skly l m ofs.
w lk f l meq
w— u z su z
psB. vsu

(9)

d rlar: ws n a wr
K gd r mlB l —
Ky. — lB + —
Kl. v — K r mmc.
—s i v Ks a mlr
v Ksn l — Kr
+ kSlu a pbm. a
mlB K lo Kz Kfy
f — kSmr. —a l
n Klnu l b a b—
—l of hz mlB K. //
wn a bc v K hz
b mlB — Kr K
dSy — Kpe rn o
e K sl — fu l a
dk co. — Ky

lwz n wl z pss
b i wd b xpnsv
l le l gl — lB of
+ —n l rlB — K
gd. sr — Kr n
— Kl. v —
mlB K e ne n
sfr a fnnx ls. e
K m — K n sm
wa l id fi —r
Kl. —n e K gl
bK — pi v —
ra mbl b slq—
mlB gd l a dk
co. n —s wa —
mlB rn l Sl b
pflB. // ppl w b —
mlB K gd n a So
r hp l b aB l gl
fu l a dk. i mlr
lll l mS ppl i K r
mlB z lq z —a n
wl i n —m. i

i a bl amzq l el
pe fm a K lB
w— a pkcr v rd
lmlo. i i n amzq
H l opn a K—l u
—q kla rd lmlo l
f— nSd ge pe!—l
Kd KSlu a KsdrB
anys & nkons. //
—r i an—r r—r
Kmn okrs—l rzf
n K gd b sd l
a dK pe. ll Ksdr
wl hpn wn — K
h b b— o d—.
—s smle hpn f
nSs wr —a r b
pK o zp. gsr
Kn sl K gd
n a dmj kdj l
— uzl pe. H
—a K gl a pe
Kl fm —r sper.

—n — gsr r of
lg l ps —s KsdrB
svq o l — Ksur.
—r r m ppl w d
n m— bq b— o
dmj K v gd z
lg z — vku i
Sl nlk. — gll v
— Kl. i n of
afK b jS a b— o
a d— n— Klar.
i i — vku —l
plK — K Kl. fm
psB spyly. dmj K
sd l a rdu pe
K b Ksdr re bgn.
s

LESSON 7

Lesson 7 presents Stenoscript Rules 31 through 36 and appropriate exercises.

Rule 31	***When you hear the*** sub ***sound, write a small*** s.

SOUND-SPELLING EXERCISE

submit sub – m – t	sml	sublet sub – l – t	sll

APPLICATION EXERCISE

subject sub – j – k	________	substitute sub – st – t – u	________
sublease sub – l – e	________	subtitle sub – t – t – l	________
submarine sub – m – r – e	________	subtract sub – t – k	________
submission sub – m – shun	________	subtropical sub – t – p – k – l	________
subscribe sub – s – k – i	________	suburb sub – b	________
subside sub – s – i	________	subway sub – w – a	________

Rule 32	*When you hear the* ad *(pronounced* add*) sound at the beginning of a word, write a small* a. *Remember, however, that for words beginning with* add *you write* ad.

SOUND-SPELLING EXERCISE

adequate
  ad – kw – t   aql

admit
  ad – m – t   aml

APPLICATION EXERCISE

adhere
  ad – h – e   ________

admire
  ad – m – i   ________

admirable
  ad – m – r – bul   ________

admission
  ad – m – shun   ________

admiration
  ad – m – r – shun   ________

advance
  ad – v – nce   ________

Note: In words that begin with *add,* write one *d.*

adding
  ad – d – ng   adg

addition
  ad – d – shun   adj

address
  ad – d – s   ads

Rule 33	*When you hear the* circ *or* circum *sound, write a capital* C.

SOUND-SPELLING EXERCISE

circle
  circ – l   Cl

circumvent
  circum – v – nt   Cv–

APPLICATION EXERCISE

circular ____________
  circ – l – r

circulate ____________
  circ – l – a

circulation ____________
  circ – l – shun

circumference ____________
  circum – f – r – nce

circumscribe ____________
  circum – s – k – i

circus ____________
  circ – s

Rule 34	*When you hear the* tive *letter group, write a small* v.

SOUND-SPELLING EXERCISE

detective *dlkv*
  d – t – k – tive

positive *pzv*
  p – z – tive

APPLICATION EXERCISE

conservative ____________
  con – s – v – tive

definitive ____________
  d – f – n – tive

formative ____________
  f – m – tive

imperative ____________
  im – p – r – tive

indicative ____________
  n – d – k – tive

inquisitive ____________
  n – kw – z – tive

lucrative ____________
  l – k – tive

prerogative ____________
  p – r – g – tive

protective ____________
  p – t – k – tive

relative ____________
  r – l – tive

selective ____________
  s – l – k – tive

talkative ____________
  t – k – tive

Rule 35	*When you hear the* lee *sound at the end of a word, write a small letter* l. *When you hear the* blee *sound at the end of a word, write* Bl.

SOUND-SPELLING EXERCISE

Word	Sounds	Shorthand
rapidly	r – p – d – lee	rpdl
annually	a – n – l – lee	anll
family	f – m – lee	fml
possibly	p – s – blee	psBl

APPLICATION EXERCISE

Word	Sounds	Shorthand
capably	k – p – blee	______
easily	e – z – lee	______
finally	f – n – l – lee	______
formerly	f – m – r – lee	______
legibly	l – j – blee	______
locally	l – k – l – lee	______
luckily	l – k – lee	______
normally	n – m – l – lee	______
quickly	kw – k – lee	______
probably	p – b – blee	______
properly	p – p – r – lee	______
secretly	c – k – t – lee	______
suddenly	s – d – n – lee	______
totally	t – t – l – lee	______

Rule 36	*When you hear the* ful *or* fully *sound, write a capital* F. *To make the* F *easy to read and write, write the numeral 7 and then cross it.*

SOUND-SPELLING EXERCISE

Word	Sounds	Shorthand
full	full	F
fully	fully	F
careful	k – a – ful	kaF
carefully	k – a – fully	kaF
watchful	w – ch – ful	wcF
watchfully	w – ch – fully	wcF

APPLICATION EXERCISE

faithful f – ith – ful	______	neglectfully n – g – k – fully	______
fearful f – e – ful	______	peacefully p – e – fully	______
gainful g – a – ful	______	thankfully ith – nk – fully	______
hopeful h – o – ful	______	trustfully t – st – fully	______
masterfully m – st – r – fully	______	wistfully w – st – fully	______
needful n – e – ful	______	wasteful w – st – ful	______

BRIEF FORM REVIEW

Write the Stenoscript outlines for the following brief forms:

association	______	particular	______
corporation	______	supervisory	______
immediate	______	representative	______
manufacturer	______	administration	______
situation	______	advantage	______
governmental	______	corporative	______
advertise	______	individual	______
company	______	particularly	______
individually	______	responsible	______
opportunity	______	approximate	______
administrative	______	organization	______
approximately	______	anticipate	______

(continued)

merchandise	________	manufactured	________
appreciation	________	suggestion	________

HIGH-FREQUENCY WORD REVIEW

Write the Stenoscript outlines for the following high-frequency words:

whose	________	question	________	on	________
answer	________	up	________	nor	________
saw	________	those	________	however	________
owe	________	whom	________	all	________
no	________	were	________	upon	________
in	________	she	________	these	________

PHRASING

Many word combinations are spoken so often that they can be written as a group. This practice is called *phrasing,* and the list of naturally occurring word phrases is almost endless. Phrasing increases your shorthand speed because you do not need to lift your pen between words. Practice the following phrases and look for them in the Reading, Writing, and Transcription Exercises in this lesson.

as soon as	zsuz	you would	uwd
I am	Im	we are	wr
I have been	Ihb	we can	wk
let us know	llsn	we have	wh
to be	lb	we have been	whb
to you	lu	we will	wl
you will	ul	we will be	wlb

CONFUSING WORDS

Word	*Definition*
weak	lacking strength
week	seven days

I am too *weak* to walk home tonight.
Our class will travel to the business show next *week*.

COMPREHENSIVE WORD REVIEW

Check your progress by writing Stenoscript outlines in your steno pad for the following words:

1. business
2. capable
3. circumstance
4. compete
5. substance
6. previous
7. descriptive
8. circular
9. attentive
10. orderly
11. consecutive
12. ever
13. believe
14. hope
15. which
16. appearance
17. cost
18. against
19. advise
20. hurry
21. price
22. repetitious
23. immediate
24. again
25. appreciate
26. reference
27. subscription
28. interview
29. opportunity
30. financial
31. executive
32. conservative
33. description
34. silently
35. helpful
36. receive
37. sister
38. capitalist
39. impossible
40. severe
41. position
42. still
43. from
44. accomplish
45. influence
46. information
47. representation
48. late
49. represent
50. expense
51. satisfy
52. consent
53. various
54. ambitious
55. incidentally
56. competitive
57. exclusively
58. quarterly
59. careful
60. most
61. piece
62. hopeful
63. after
64. best
65. stand
66. once
67. compel
68. carry
69. annually
70. since
71. raise
72. advocate *(v)*

QUICK COMMA REVIEW

Recalling the punctuation rules from the front of the book, use a comma

m. to set off abbreviations that follow a person's name.

Jerome Powers, Ph.D.
Denise Watts, D.D.S.
Cecil Mills, M.D.
Sister Anne Arnold, O.S.F.
Raymond Lloyd, Esq.

n. to separate an individual's first name from the last name when the name is given in inverted order.

O'Day, Jane   VanderRoest, Duane

WRITING EXERCISE

Practice writing these sentences in Stenoscript in your steno pad:

1. Their representative suggested that we install a costly substitute for the defective part.
2. We have not previously advertised this admirable product, but we are now advocating a massive sales campaign.
3. The circulation of that newspaper is normally less than 10,000, but after the terrible crime it approximated 50,000, excluding home subscriptions.
4. It is imperative that the information be distributed both locally and nationally so that the situation can be adequately evaluated by the people before the elections.
5. The detective kept a watchful eye on the subway, hopeful of finally catching the runaway children.
6. The adverse reaction of the public to the protective tax finally provoked a change in policy.
7. Locally, the new candidate was favored, but nationally he was hopelessly behind.
8. He accomplished the difficult task easily, in fact masterfully.
9. The beautiful circus performer advanced fearlessly along the rope.
10. Luckily, the subtropical climate is admirably suited to her delicate health.

READING, WRITING, AND TRANSCRIPTION EXERCISES

(1)

dmr sm—: wr hp
l nfm u —l r
xkv Kml hz apv
u ppzl. wl b rd
l og w o u pjk
zsuz a Klk hz b
si. a lv rf
Klk ac -s llr.
pz xmn i + llsn
i — lm. r sl
l u. wk -n g
imd l a fnl vj. //
ma I sa f msf
+ l — ofsr v —
co —l w ap -s
op l w w— a
mn v u fi rply
o sc a w-e pjk.
wr lkg f l a
nSg + pdkv rlypp
w— u gu. uvl

(2)

j: wr rug l rm
u v — lm. v u
Klk w— s wc Kl
f sl Kpj v u w
b — — v nx W.
wr Ksn —l uln
me — lm. v —
Klk si whn yl
c u skc o pn.
i i r kSm l wn
sklkr. i w -g -a
r n dnyr v dflg.
-r r fgl wa n
wc wk hp r spir
me -r obgj l s. //
ma w avz u l
vzl r ofs fal su
o —l w ma xmn

Ray — ryn. f —
dla & php. ofr sm
sug. wr ppa l
me w— u l u
Kons b i i mprv
— l i b n — ne
fcr. vlu

fnyg. w —g r
kplg l me u hi
S—. v gll n
mtrl & dzi. pz
k n b d llsn n
avs o — l wlb
ppa l sv u. su

(3)

dmr sm—: — nu
smpl. v kplg — spo lu
ag rsl h fnll arv
n r zoru. w —g
—a r skl wl u r
lkg f. —a r smpl.
v a kplg — l i
espsl ma f us n
So & ofs wa lfk i
spk l b hv. ll
uh a dkmnag Knll
& w n i i mprv
— l u b gi slkv
n u cys v rq. &

(4)

ds: 4 M ag — s
l u o dp a o n
— am v 52^{53} wc
z lb zp l — ads
zon o — nkz bl.
— ssg l rcv a ak
v — o w— a
kp v i nkz. lS
M — rcv a Sa
fm u blg dp
zog — l — Sl o
— am v 52^{53}.
— rsp b rug &
spag — l — pa

f — o' h b
nkz n m orynl
ltr. sr —n Ihb
rcvq bl rghl fm
u blq dp= wc
ad NS cj l—
orynl sm. sr m
ck Ke — bq lq
ag Im l a ls
l n y u klnu
l bl e. // l u
pz lk nl —s
mlr kaf w— u
blq dp=? Im
hof —l ul rzv
—s sil su + Sml l
l a nu Sa— zoq
—l m ak— w
u hz b pa n 7.
wl

(5)

dms mlr: —z u

f u rs— o' f a
qe=sz bd. llb
dlvr z pms. //
Im laq —s op
l nkz a Clr dkq
— bdq —l i o sa
l —s li. u ma
w— l la avf v
—s spx sa wc w
h anll n —fl.
pi l q bk l nml
su o i i mprv
—l u ak qkl i uwd
li l h sm v —s
fi bdq l bgn pi.
ul pb3l nls —l
w nku n —s sa
a qe=sz elklk bql.
—s hz b av pplr
nmbr w— r kSmr.
wh h fu kp.
ag — svs i
gv. n spi v —

fk — l whb Kyq
—z bql n Sk s,
1985. — bql i
bf b— + k n 5
lvl Klr. // wr
lwz pz l sv u
n wlev wa wk.
ma w pss u o
f bdq su? vlu

bd bdq + wa rdk. //
w rec — l u vzt
— h— Kb rqlrl +
la avj v r olmpk=
sz pu. // fnll wr pz
l lk u z a mmbr
+ ho — l ul la 7
avj v r fsll. wvl

(6)

d mmbr: — nkz
Clr dk — akvl
pgm v — bq lwn
h Kb wc uh jS
jyn. w avka — l
ec nu mmbr Uq
a Kpe fzkl xmnj
bf bq r pgm. — n
l v r h— xp:
l rec a pgm v
xsz Se b: + msj
kkla l b hpj n

(7)

dms bxtr: i i w
snse pzr — l I lk
u z a nu cj kSmr
l — fafd dp
So. ul f — l lo
r So hz gal xp
s, i z f 76 y.
aq l r mds i Sl
v — sa qll — l
en s r fi rply. //
fl + efz k:
l avz u o l v r
nu pdk li. gv s

a Kl o k n su f
dp alnj l l v u
ho ne. // z a cj
kSmr u r nlll l
uz r kvn— ml
nSl. f pag u
bl. —s me —l
u ma b p l 2h$
w— v mds a M
& pa onl 10$ ps
nS o r Ml nSl
pn. // r hj smanl
fncr sa hz jS bq.
w n u l f r
slkj oSgl blj.
dp n su & ll s
gl psnll ag.
vsu

(8)

dmr sm—: n o
l sSnja u ka aq
m k— rb= jnz l
m rqSq —l u f
l e a kp v —
sle klk. // akq l
m rk. u pp z
sdvr lS M b mcl
ks—. a nu klk z
—n rln & — a— &
nu slll w nku.
l —l u l ape z
—o — 2 p. w pz
& fl —l —s pp spl
z avj l b—. // —s
m k— z lll spz
wn e rcv lD a
spna rqiq m l
ape n k mx W
aq —s mtr. w
h u l hl —
mtr objkol r r
—n n a sjkv mnr
n fk w h b hoj
v slq l dfrj. O

v K. aprl i l
b mpsB l d —s. ||
n or l sml l u
wz & me u n K
nx W —d mS as u
l s— e a Kp v —
Klk. —s nfo i v
Ks avaB —u o r
ss b u Kopry wd
xpdi a fnl rzly.
su

(9)

dmr bkr: z —d pms
l r meq LS W —d
m sq u sprll slk
Kp v r pbky lg r
w— r od Klq. w
r pzl ppaq a nu
Klq. —d l f flkp
v — kp bf i i s—
l — pr. || —
pnspl sjk —l w

dks wr u w he
z — psbll v u
a rq sn bk f s
o a ryll bss. —s
v Ks wd b sjk l
apvl b r edbl b.
af — nssy apvl
w Kd ezl da p a
llr v age —l wd
pml u oq l sle z
mbrl. —s wd b
ez l arny. r lyr
hz dan p a rf
df l sml l u f
u ksdry. pz s—
s u raky zouz
psB. —n w K ppa
l dks i n dla.
e r ru e o Kl e
Klk l u Kony. || i
z bul nyyB l h u
he. —d d ho—l
CSy l pml s l

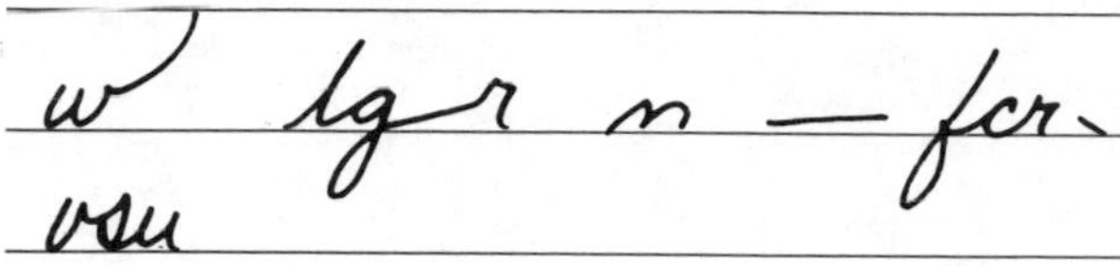

LESSON

8

Lesson 8 presents Stenoscript Rules 37 through 40, including the Stenoscript abbreviations for times and directions, and appropriate exercises.

Rule 37	*When you hear the* un *sound at the beginning of a word, write a small* u.

SOUND-SPELLING EXERCISE

unable un – a – bul	uaB		unofficial un – o – f – shul	uofx
unnecessary un – n – s – s – ree	unnsy		untimely un – t – i – lee	util

APPLICATION EXERCISE

unbend un – b – nd	__________	unless un – l – s	__________
uncommon un – k – m – n	__________	unload un – l – o	__________
uncut un – k – t	__________	unnatural un – n – ch – r – l	__________
uneasy un – e – z	__________	unrest un – r – st	__________
unequal un – e – kw – l	__________	unsafe un – s – a	__________
unfed un – f – d	__________	untidy un – t – d	__________
ungracious un – g – shus	__________	until un – t – l	__________
uninterested un – inter – st – ed	__________		

Rule 38	*When you hear the* trans *sound at the beginning of a word, write a capital* T.

SOUND-SPELLING EXERCISE

transact
trans – a – k ____Tak____

transit
trans – t ____Tt____

transparency
trans – p – r – n – c ____Tprnc____

APPLICATION EXERCISE

transaction
trans – a – k – shun ________

transfuse
trans – f – z ________

transpose
trans – p – z ________

transfer
trans – f – r ________

transform
trans – f – m ________

translate
trans – l – a ________

transmit
trans – m – t ________

transparent
trans – p – r – nt ________

transplant
trans – p – nt ________

transportation
trans – p – t – shun ________

Rule 39a	*When you hear the* ow *sound, write a small* w.

SOUND-SPELLING EXERCISE

doubt
d – ow – t ____dwt____

loud
l – ow – d ____lwd____

how
h – ow ____hw____

APPLICATION EXERCISE

allow
a – l – ow ________

aloud
a – l – ow – d ________

arouse
a – r – ow – z ________

brown
b – ow – n ________

council ____________
k – ow – n – s – l

crowd ____________
k – ow – d

down ____________
d – ow – n

mouth ____________
m – ow – ith

now ____________
n – ow

ounce ____________
ow – nce

voucher ____________
v – ow – ch – r

vowel ____________
v – ow – l

Rule 39b	*When the* ow *sound occurs before the* nt *or* nd *sound, do not write the* w *for the* ow *sound. Instead, write a dash for the* nt *or* nd *sound.*

SOUND-SPELLING EXERCISE

account ak
a – k – nt

found f
f – nd

APPLICATION EXERCISE

around ____________
a – r – nd

bound ____________
b – nd

couch ____________
k – ow – ch

counsel ____________
k – ow – n – s – l

discount ____________
dis – k – nt

encounter ____________
n – k – nt – r

endow ____________
n – d – ow

flower ____________
f – ow – r

foul ____________
f – ow – l

fountain ____________
f – nt – n

frown ____________
f – ow – n

lounge ____________
l – ow – n – j

mountain ____________
m – nt – n

power ____________
p – ow – r

renown ____________
r – n – ow – n

sound ____________
s – nd

surround ____________
s – r – nd

town ____________
t – ow – n

Rule 40	***Memorize the Stenoscript abbreviations for times and directions.***

a. Days of the week

Sunday	Sn	Thursday	Th
Monday	Mn	Friday	Fr
Tuesday	Ts	Saturday	St
Wednesday	Wd		

b. Months of the year

January	Ja	May	Ma	September	Sp
February	Fb	June	Ju	October	Oc
March	Mr	July	Jl	November	Nv
April	Ap	August	Ag	December	Dc

c. Times of day

a.m.	a	p.m.	p

d. Directions

north	N	northeast	NE
south	S	northwest	NW
east	E	southeast	SE
west	W	southwest	SW
western	W^n	southwestern	SW^n

BRIEF FORM REVIEW

opportunity	______	organize	______
particular	______	represent	______
responsible	______	satisfy	______
situation	______	specify	______
company	______	corporate	______
government	______	immediate	______
individual	______	information	______
manufacture	______	merchandise	______
accompany	______	accomplish	______
acknowledge	______	administer	______
appreciate	______	approximate	______
associate	______	business	______
advertised	______	anticipation	______
recommended	______	advantages	______
suggested	______	supervised	______

PHRASING

Practice the following phrases until you can write them quickly and accurately. Look for these and other phrases in the Reading, Writing, and Transcription Exercises in this lesson. (Additional phrases are listed in the Index of Phrases in the Appendix.)

have been	hb	for your	fu
have had	hh	Thank you for your	gufu
for you	fu	Thank you for your letter	gufullr

(continued)

will be lb

you will be ulb

you should uzd

CONFUSING WORDS

Word	*Definition*
whose	possessive
who's	who is

Whose computer is malfunctioning?
Who's that student with the red coat and black hat?

QUICK COMMA REVIEW

Recalling the punctuation rules from the front of the book, use a comma

o. to separate numbers into groups of thousands. Do *not* use commas to separate groups of thousands in years or policy, page, telephone, or serial numbers.

456,876	year 1983
policy number 2234590	page 1004
telephone 555-1121	serial number 4590453

p. to set off contrasting expressions.

Arthur, not Sam, will give the keynote address.

COMPREHENSIVE WORD REVIEW

Check your progress by writing Stenoscript outlines in your steno pad for the following words:

1. now
2. unnecessary
3. January
4. June
5. 10 a.m.
6. Tuesday
7. transferred
8. carefully
9. about
10. surrounding
11. approximately
12. untimely
13. March
14. lately
15. northeast
16. Wednesday
17. unlikely
18. August
19. expensive
20. northwest
21. after
22. around
23. opportunity
24. sublet
25. December
26. proud
27. week

28. wonderful
29. July
30. voucher
31. Monday
32. translation
33. somehow
34. April
35. previously
36. Friday
37. disallow
38. apparently
39. 7 p.m.
40. southeast
41. loudly
42. month
43. finally
44. May
45. transparent
46. without
47. recount
48. particular
49. relatively
50. November
51. abundance
52. day
53. circumstance
54. adequate
55. unequaled
56. circular
57. September
58. thankful
59. transportation
60. Saturday
61. transpose
62. substitute
63. announcement
64. February
65. endowment
66. year
67. warehouse
68. October
69. Sunday
70. attentively
71. southwest
72. Thursday

WRITING EXERCISE

Practice writing these sentences in Stenoscript in your steno pad:

1. On Monday, January 24, we will announce our decision on the awarding of contracts.
2. Most of the people in the crowd came from the surrounding towns.
3. A faulty transmission made the car unsafe for driving.
4. The men hope to finish unloading the merchandise by 3 p.m. on Saturday.
5. Until we have received all of the necessary information, we are unable to complete the transaction.
6. In about two weeks, our company will transfer all of our records to our new offices.
7. Because you have seniority, it is unlikely that you will be transferred.
8. Our special excursion rate includes round-trip transportation as well as hotel accommodations for nine days.
9. Unless he encounters unforeseen opposition, he should be able to persuade the town council to accept his proposal.
10. Public transportation on the south side of the city is unreliable.

READING, WRITING, AND TRANSCRIPTION EXERCISES

(1)

dmr bwn: —qufullr
v Oc 24. w d ma a
mSa o — Tply cj
& w ap u Klg —s
err l r alnj. // r
rk. hb ajS & u ak—
nw zo. a Kdl v
17$. s

(2)

dms Kwl: wh rcv
u llr v Dc 3 n wc
u avz s —l —
Kwc & ca u rcv
lS W arv n dmj
Kdj. w nlfi — xps
co v —s sil & —a
aml —l — fncr
z dmj n Il. // rS
azu —l — dmj pe.
lb rpa w q ne
KS l u. wwd H
ap mo nfo ag —
Kdj v — fncr o —l
w ma fi r Ka f
dmj. // —qufu asSj
n —s mtr. vlu

(3)

ds: nkz i u Sa
zoq a upa blj v
306$. —s fqr nku
— Takj v Ja 5 &
Mr 10. drq — pS
Y wh ma m alwj
f ufcnl CSj. —l
pv — pmp pa — v
—s bl. H sj wh
rcv n pa & hh n
w fm u n — pS
M w r qi Ksn. //

uls w he fm u
wn — W wl b
fs l ln — mlr
V l r lyz. ul

(4)

d bl: — anl meg
f co samn n bSn
& — srq ara lb
hd Fb 11 12 & 13 l
— als hll n bSn. 11
bkz — D lb v bz
l l me lb sv n
— hll dlq ru. ulb
as l slk u mnu
n avs l avyd ne
unssy dla n fu
svs. 11 arnj f fu
Tply & ru rzvj r
b hl b my lwnr.
uzd b heg fm r
wn — nx fu D. 11
wr l lkq f l c

u he nx M. s

(5)

ds: w rgl l nfm
u — l — pwr. hll
l uaB l rzv a
ru fu o Sl & Sn
Ma 1 & 2. 11 wlb
mo — n hp l almp
l ma rzvj n an r
hll. H og l —
pzs v 2 lg kvnj n
— sl o oz D. l
l ulil — l suB
akmdj lb avaB. w
sug — l l l l
psB u pSpo u vzl
ull — flog W wn
— hll l b ls
Kwd. 11 sr l lvl
arnj. dp o —
da v u lp wr
agr l he fm u

af —s mbr. ul

hz b so n — pS. ul

(6)

ds: m co r h lB
Ip9 —r mds rpdl
l sml lwn. w v
Nmdl lkq co h ma
a spx Sd v —s
pbm. —u arny.
w m sml b
rlB lkq co wr nw
aB l gv Vn svs
l ne lwn wn 3h
me v — sl. ull
—s pn z w- O b
s i lk svrl D l
ma dlvy l sm
v —z lwn. // w
—g u l le —s
nu svs. pz kl
o s l hp u —
nx le u h a zp
q l ne lwn wa svs

(7)

j: —s i l rm—
u v — mbr w
dks l r lkl meg
o Ts. z D ld u —n
a drkv rg9 akrl rk.
mS b ize imd. uls
—s i d D fe —l
srx pbm l arz. //
n a avry W w nu Kpe
h d v Taks. i i n
uuzl f a nmbr v
—m l Kla err. m
sc err r d l uld
nakrl o kals rk.
— pbm z n ga
ull rs M wn—
vlu v r bz nke
m-. pz ma ke l
l v u mpye. —

mpl v Krkl Ikg
sa fgr KS eSml
kSmr j ads + o o.//
a V pn f mpvg co
m-d n -s mlr
i bdl ne. I ho
-l l v u l -g
ag -s kaj. pz
sml u ida l e n
rig bf - Ng ryml
meg n Ag. -gufu
Kopry. uvl

(8)

ds: w h jS rcv u
lbr da Ih Ma 20
1988. w US -l r
rs- zp- v gswa rc
u n usl Kdj. z u
ma n w la uizl
Ka n pkg r pdk.
wr uaB l grnl
-l -a r ubaB. H

w fe -l r m-d.
v pkjg ma baj
ulel. w nw asu -l
u o z dmj n Il.
n dwt i z hl n
a uyz mnr. -guf
llg s n ag -s mlr
o pmpl. // lu alw
s nw l rpa u o
w- an-r? w k
vwc f i arvl n blr
Kdj. -r l v Ks
b n adjl cj l u.
u l Sl rcv - dk
alw o u oryml o.
uls u nfm s
o-rwz w l s- -
rpa- imd. alw ag
2 W n Il. - nu
o zd rc u o o ag
- 5 v Ju. n adj
w l nw Ifr u lbr
l r Kp- dp. -a

l — n nvSga — rzn
f — s ufcnl aksd . ||
w snsel rgl —
uavrjdB dla n — s
Takj . — qufu USq .
vlu

(9)

ds: n rsps l u llr
da Ma 12 1988 wr
sq l u svrl v
r bzu . — a dki
n dla r nle li v
fm egp + spi . w
ho — l u l f amg
— mdl dki sm
— l l me u ne . ||
u ndka — l u opry
rgi a uuzll lj nmbr
v pu rer + o r
pwry fm mzey . — rf
u lb gd l ln ag
— jnrs dk . w

nw alw o sc pcs .
dla v r alwy pn
K b f n l v
— bzu mny abv .
u ma lo b lgB
f spx cznl pi
rdkj . l la avj v
cznl dk . H u
or mS b Tml l s
bf Jl l v — s Y .
i u h ne Q pz
Kl r lkl rpl —
Nz ara ofs . e l
skzl a vzl w — u
l u Kvns . || ull ls
Y w d n ofr rpa
+ mnlns svs f r
pdk . z u ma lrd
n w nw h a lj
Sf v svs rp . — z
mn r spxl la l
svs l mdl n r
li . — a opra n

m st. & lwn. aks
— knly . i i ulil
—l u l h mc lB
w— r sl— pdk.
H u ne n b uez
ag —l . i a pbm
dz K p smpl Kl
— neS svs ofs.
l v r rp l pmpl
K l u pa v bz l
hp u. l v —
svs ofs r opn fm
9a ull 5 p Mn
—u Sl. // f u Kons
—l m nkzg svrl
Tmll fm. l b uz-
n pag u o. uz
a sprl fm f ec
mdl nmbr. b zu
l ndka — g l.
u wz l pcs. —n
rln — fm. l r
ma ofs. w l —
arny f u o l
b Tp- l u zsuz
psB. // —gu v mc
f u rs— ltr v
ngy & f u pS
bz. w lk f l
svg u ag n—
ne fcr. vlu

LESSON 9 Using Your Shorthand Skills

Now that you have mastered the theory of Stenoscript, you are ready to develop your dictation and transcription skills. This chapter provides practical advice on how to take dictation, transcribe your notes quickly, and use shorthand in notetaking.

TAKING DICTATION

You must practice taking dictation every day. This is extremely important because it is the only way to attain your speed goal.

You must continuously strive to take dictation at a speed somewhat higher than your ability. When you can take dictation at a given speed with only three to five errors, you should increase the dictation speed ten words per minute. You will gradually improve your ability to coordinate what you hear with what you write.

It is best to take shorthand from timed records or tapes or from a person who is experienced in giving dictation. You will find that an inexperienced person will not dictate evenly or accurately.

Your first speed goal should be 60 words per minute. The average person writes longhand at approximately 40 words per minute. As you attempt to put Stenoscript theory into practice, at first you will probably find that you cannot take the dictation at 60 words per minute. After five or ten one-minute timed tests, however, you will begin to increase both your accuracy and speed. When you attain the speed of 60 words per minute and are making only three to five errors, you should increase your goal to 70 words per minute and thereafter increase it each time you master a new speed level.

When taking dictation, write as quickly and accurately as you can. Omit words that are difficult for you; you will learn those words in time. Concentrating on a single word during dictation could cause you to lose an entire sentence!

The purpose of all shorthand systems is to minimize the amount of writing and to increase your ability to write more words per minute. With regular practice and constant use, many Stenoscript students are able to take dictation at the rate of 80 to 100 words per minute.

TRANSCRIBING STENOSCRIPT

Of all shorthand systems, Stenoscript is probably the easiest to transcribe, and you should have no difficulty learning it. You must, however, remember the following points. They will help you transcribe your notes more rapidly.

In Stenoscript, vowels are written *only at the beginning or end of a base word.* When you see a vowel written within a word, you know that the vowel begins or ends a base word to which a prefix or suffix has been added. For example, *r, d, u,* or *T* before a vowel could stand respectively for the prefix *re, dis, un,* or *trans. B, g, l, r,* or *v* after a vowel could represent the suffix *able, ing, ly, er,* or *tive.* You should *figure out the base word first and then add the prefix or suffix.*

Now consider the following examples:

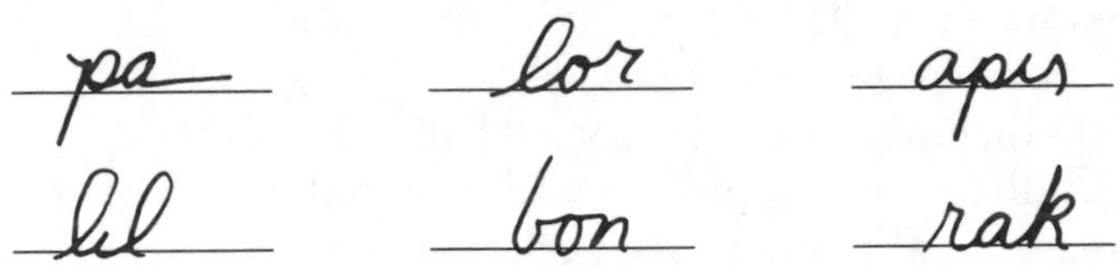

In the first example, if you transcribe only as far as *pa*, you have the base word *pay*. By adding the suffix represented by the dash, you have the word *payment.* The second word transcribed as far as *lo* gives you the base word *low,* and adding the suffix *r* gives you *lower.*

Transcribing the other words, you first get *apply*, then *appliance; like,* then *likely; broke,* then *broken.* In the last example, you transcribe the base word *act* and add the prefix *re* to get the word *react.*

As you have learned, there are two kinds of words whose Stenoscript outlines end in a vowel: (1) words that end in a vowel sound (such as *pay* or *low*) and (2) words in which the final single consonant sound is preceded by a long-vowel sound (such as *broke* or *like*). The following list presents possible final consonants for words to which the long-vowel rule applies.

b
c (as in *lace*)
d
f
g (as in *dog*, but not as in *cage*)
k
l
m
n
p

q (as in *antique*)
r (with *a* as in *care*, *e* as in *fear*, *o* as in *more*, *u* as in *pure*)
s (as in *case*, but not as in *tease*)
t

This list will help you to transcribe words in the second category quickly and accurately. In the Stenoscript sentence below, for example, if you could not transcribe the word *fe* as *fee*, you would consult the list and find that by adding a single consonant sound at the end you could form *feed, feel, fear, feat, feet, flee, fleet,* or *free.* (Don't forget about an *l* or *r* that might have dropped out!)

Looking at the word in the context of the sentence, however, would tell you that *fe* must logically be *feel.* The sentence reads, "*The boy does not feel well.*"

Now consider the following sentence:

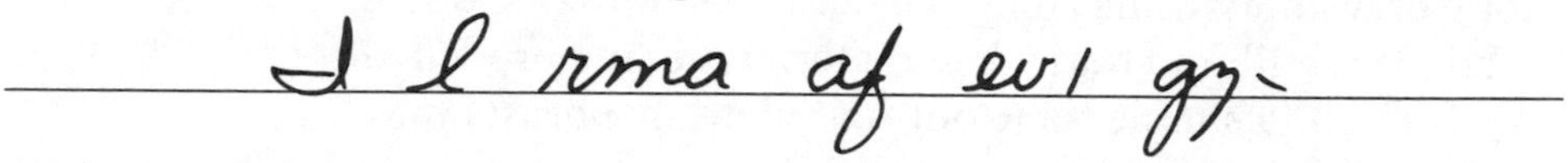

The list will show you that possible transcriptions for *rma* include *remain, remade,* and *remake.* From the context of the sentence, you would immediately know that the word must be *remain.* Thus the transcription reads, "*I will remain after everyone goes.*"

Remember that this list identifies the consonant *sound* and *not the spelling* of the word ending. One sound may have several spellings. For example, the sound of *a* plus *d* may be spelled *ade* (as in *made*) or *aid* (as in *maid*). When transcribing a difficult word, try adding each consonant sound to the final long vowel of the word and then try the word in the context of the sentence. Remember that you pronounce the *a* as in *pay*, the *e* as in *fee*, the *i* as in *pie*, the *o* as in *show*, and the *u* as in *shoe* or *cue.*

PHRASING

Connecting the words of commonly used phrases will increase the speed of experienced shorthand writers. After you have mastered the theory of Stenoscript and learned to take dictation accurately, you will find phrasing valuable for writing familiar, frequently used groups of words.

Phrasing generally follows the standard Stenoscript outlines except that the words in the phrase are connected. For example, the phrase, "*Thank you for your letter*" would be written

NOTETAKING IN STENOSCRIPT

Stenoscript is invaluable for notetaking as well as dictation. Whether you are taking notes in the classroom, at a lecture, or at a meeting, you must use efficient notetaking techniques. The following basic principles will help you to improve the quality of your notes:

1. ***Listen carefully.*** This is the first step in effective notetaking. To take meaningful notes, you must understand what is being said. If your notes are solely for your own use, wait until a speaker has expressed a complete thought and then summarize it in your own words. At other times, you must note *exactly* what has been said. In the classroom, for example, the teacher may indicate that a particular statement should be copied word for word. When your notes are to be used for an official purpose, such as the minutes of a meeting, record the speaker's phrases rather than your own summary. Unless a statement must be recorded verbatim, do not worry about using complete sentences or taking down every word. In fact, you will find that when material is being presented in a very orderly fashion, a simple topic outline (word or phrase) may best suit your needs.
2. ***Take down only the main points and important details of the material presented.*** Look for verbal clues to help you recognize the important points. Phrases such as "*In the first place,*" "*I would like to call your attention to . . .* ," and "*In conclusion, . . .* " indicate that the statements that follow may be worth noting.
3. ***Edit your notes.*** Reread your notes while the material is still fresh in your mind. You can then rewrite any carelessly formed outlines or write out words for those abbreviated outlines that might later prove difficult to read. You may also wish to underline key ideas, add or eliminate certain details, or completely reorganize your notes. (This would be particularly useful for notes taken at a meeting when no definite agenda had been followed, for class notes involving a great deal of discussion, or for lecture notes when the material had not been presented in an organized manner.)

In addition to these basic principles, the following practical hints will help you take more efficient notes:

1. Be sure that you have the necessary materials. A ballpoint pen is preferable to a pencil. The point will not break or wear down, and you can save time by crossing out errors rather than erasing them. Be sure to have several pens in case one runs out of ink!

2. Check to see that you have enough paper in your notebook or steno pad. Overestimate your needs to be on the safe side.
3. Use a firm surface to write on. If a table is not available, use a clipboard or the hard cover of a notebook.
4. Decide on a means of identifying the topic and place this identification at the top of each page of your notes. Notes for a biology class might have "Bio" written at the top of the page. "PR2" could keynote pages for the second in a series of public relations meetings. Dating and numbering your pages will be an additional means of identification if one page becomes separated from the others. Label your note pages either *before or after* the actual notetaking. Do not waste time labeling pages when you should be concentrating on what is being said.
5. Whenever possible, try to find out in advance the topic or topics to be discussed. Then devise your own Stenoscript abbreviations for certain words, names, and special terms that you know will be mentioned frequently. For example, if you are attending a conference on the training of unskilled workers, you might use abbreviations similar to the following: *Uw* for *unskilled worker, T* for *train, FG* for *federal government,* and *Pn* for *private industry.*
6. If you are taking notes at a meeting where the speakers' names must be recorded, try to obtain a list of participants beforehand and learn who they are so that you can identify them during the meeting. Devise special Stenoscript abbreviations for their names and a system to indicate when each speaker is speaking.
7. A good way to practice and to build your skill is to take notes while listening to panel discussions, lectures, and interview programs on radio or television.

These are only a few of the ways to improve your notetaking skills. As you become more experienced, you will discover your own shortcuts for more efficient and accurate notetaking.

Appendix

INDEX OF HIGH-FREQUENCY WORDS

INDEX OF BRIEF FORMS

INDEX OF PHRASES

INDEX OF TIMES AND DIRECTIONS

SALUTATIONS AND CLOSINGS OF LETTERS

ABBREVIATIONS FOR THE UNITED STATES AND U.S. TERRITORIES

ABBREVIATIONS FOR CANADIAN PROVINCES AND TERRITORIES

ABBREVIATIONS FOR METRIC MEASUREMENTS

SUMMARY OF STENOSCRIPT RULES

INDEX OF HIGH-FREQUENCY WORDS

a	a
about	ab
after	af
again	ag
against	ag
all	l
am	m
an	a
and	&
answer	A
any	ne
are	r
as	z
at	t
be	b
been	b
began	bg
begin	bg
beginning	bg
begun	bg
being	b
but	b
buy	b
bye	b
by	b
came	k
can	k
come	k
coming	k
day	D
did	d
do	d
does	dz
doing	d
done	d
due	d
even	ev
ever	ev
every	ev
for	f
from	fm
go	g
goes	gz
going	g
gone	g
had	h
has	hz
have	h
having	h
he	e
her	r
hers	r
him	m
his	z
hour	r
however	H
I	I
if	i
in	n
is	i
it	i
its	i
know	n
many	m
me	e
mine	m
month	M
my	m
neither	n

never	nv	seeing	c	was	z
no	n	seen	c	we	w
none	n	she	z	week	W
nor	n	so	o	well	l
not	n	that	—l	were	w
of	v	the	—	where	wa
off	of	their	—r	which	wc
often	of	there	—r	who	w
on	o	these	—z	whom	w
or	o	they	—a	whose	wz
our	r	this	—o	why	y
ours	r	those	—oz	will	l
out	O	to	l	with	w—
over	V	too	l	without	wO
owe	o	under	U	year	Y
question	Q	up	p	you	u
saw	s	upon	pn	your	u
says	sz	us	s	yours	u
see	c	very	v		

INDEX OF BRIEF FORMS

accompany	ac
accomplish	ac
acknowledge	ak
administer	adm
advantage	avj
advertise	adv
anticipate	ant
appreciate	ap
approximate	apx
associate	as
business	bz
company	co
corporate	crp
government	gvt
immediate	imd
individual	ndv
information	nfo
manufacture	mf
merchandise	mds
opportunity	op
organize	og
particular	prt
recommend	rec
represent	rp
responsible	rsp
satisfy	st
situation	sit
specify	spc
suggest	sug
supervise	spv

INDEX OF PHRASES

The following list presents 137 phrases in alphabetical order. These are only a few of the many word combinations that can be naturally phrased to increase writing speed.

about the	ao—
all of them	lvm
are not	rn
as good as	zgdz
as great as	zgaz
as low as	zloz
as many as	zmnz
as much as	zmcz
as to	zt
as you	zu
as well as	zlz
at all	tl
at any	tne
at any time	tnet
at once	tws
at that	t t
did not	dn
does not	dzn
for the	f—
for us	fs
from the	fm—
from you	fmu
from your	fmu
have been able	hbaB
he is	ei
he had	eh
he was not	ezn
he will	el
I do not	Idn
I do not believe	Idnblv
I do not know	Idnn
I do not see	Idnc
I had	Ih
I have	Ih
if you are	iur
if you will	iul
if the	i—
in due course	ndKs
in due time	ndt
in his	nz
in reply	nrpi
in which	nwc

into the	nl	that this	ls
is not	sn	there are	rr
it may be	imab	there is	rs
it is not	tsn	there is not	rsn
it must be	imSb	they do not	adn
it was not	izn	they do not know	adnn
more than	mon	they had	ah
must be	mSb	through the	u
of it	vt	to ask	las
of its	vt	to be	lb
of their	vr	to draw	lda
of them	vm	to get	lgt
of these	vz	to give	lgv
of this	vs	to go	lg
of which	vwc	to honor	lonr
on our	or	to keep	lke
on the	o	to know	ln
on you	ou	to make	lma
on your	ou	to me	le
over the	O	to mean	lme
should be	zdb	to meet	lme
should be able	zdbaB	to my	lm
that is	ls	to our	lr
that they	la	to pay	lpa

to place	lpa
to say	lsa
to see	lc
to ship	lzp
to take	lla
to this	l-s
to which	lwc
to work	lw
was not	zn
we are	wr
we are not	wrn
we can	wk
we do not	wdn
we do not believe	wdnblv
we had	wh
we have	wh
we have been	whb
we have not	whn
we may	wma
we must	wmS
we shall	wzl
we shall be	wzlb
we shall not	wzln
we should	wzd
we will	wl
we will not	wln
we would	wwd
what to do	wlld
when the	wn-
which have	wch
which is	wci
who have	wh
will be able	lbaB
will you	lu
with us	w-s
with that	w-l
with the	w-
would be able	wdbaB
you are	ur
you do not	udn
you do not know	udnn
you had	uh
you have	uh
you know	un
your letter	ullr
you may	uma
you would	uwd

INDEX OF TIMES AND DIRECTIONS

Days

Sunday	Sn	Thursday	Th
Monday	Mn	Friday	Fr
Tuesday	Ts	Saturday	St
Wednesday	Wd		

Months

January	Ja	July	Jl
February	Fb	August	Ag
March	Mr	September	Sp
April	Ap	October	Oc
May	Ma	November	Nv
June	Ju	December	Dc

Times of Day

a.m.	a	p.m.	p

Directions

north	N	northeast	NE
south	S	northwest	Nw
east	E	southeast	SE
west	W	southwest	Sw
western	Wn	southwestern	Swn

SALUTATIONS AND CLOSINGS OF LETTERS

Salutations

Dear	d	Gentlemen	j
Dear Sir	ds	Dear Mr.	dmr
Dear Madam	dm	Dear Miss	dmi
Dear Ms.	dmz	Dear Mrs.	dms
Ladies and Gentlemen	l & j		

Complimentary Closings

Cordially	c	Yours sincerely	us
Cordially yours	cu	Yours truly	ul
Respectfully	r	Yours very truly	uvl
Sincerely	s	Very truly yours	vlu
Sincerely yours	su		

ABBREVIATIONS FOR THE UNITED STATES AND U.S. TERRITORIES

Alabama (AL)	Al	Michigan (MI)	Mi
Alaska (AK)	Ak	Minnesota (MN)	Mn
Arizona (AZ)	Az	Mississippi (MS)	Ms
Arkansas (AR)	Ar	Missouri (MO)	Mo
California (CA)	Ca	Montana (MT)	Mt
Colorado (CO)	Co	Nebraska (NE)	Ne
Connecticut (CT)	Ct	Nevada (NV)	Nv
Delaware (DE)	De	New Hampshire (NH)	Nh
District of Columbia (DC)	Dc	New Jersey (NJ)	Nj
Florida (FL)	Fl	New Mexico (NM)	Nm
Georgia (GA)	Ga	New York (NY)	Ny
Hawaii (HI)	Hi	North Carolina (NC)	Nc
Idaho (ID)	Id	North Dakota (ND)	Nd
Illinois (IL)	Il	Ohio (OH)	Oh
Indiana (IN)	In	Oklahoma (OK)	Ok
Iowa (IA)	Ia	Oregon (OR)	Or
Kansas (KS)	Ks	Pennsylvania (PA)	Pa
Kentucky (KY)	Ky	Rhode Island (RI)	Ri
Louisiana (LA)	La	South Carolina (SC)	Sc
Maine (ME)	Me	South Dakota (SD)	Sd
Maryland (MD)	Md	Tennessee (TN)	Tn
Massachusetts (MA)	Ma	Texas (TX)	Tx

Utah (UT)	Ut	Wyoming (WY)	Wy
Vermont (VT)	Vt	Canal Zone (CZ)	Cz
Virginia (VA)	Va	Guam (GU)	Gu
Washington (WA)	Wa	Puerto Rico (PR)	pr
West Virginia (WV)	Wv	Virgin Islands (VI)	Vi
Wisconsin (WI)	Wi		

CANADIAN PROVINCES AND TERRITORIES

Alberta (AB)	Ab	Nova Scotia (NS)	NS
British Columbia (BC)	Bc	Ontario (ON)	On
Manitoba (MB)	Mb	Prince Edward Island (PE)	pe
New Brunswick (NB)	Nb	Quebec (PQ)	Pq
Newfoundland (NF)	Nf	Saskatchewan (SK)	Sk
Northwest Territories (NT)	Nt	Yukon Territory (YT)	Yt

METRIC MEASUREMENTS

	meter (length) m	liter (capacity) l	gram (weight) g
kilo	klm	kll	klg
hecto	hkm	hkl	hkg
deca	dkm	dkl	dkg
deci	dsm	dsl	dsg
centi	sm	sl	sg
milli	mlm	mll	mlg
micro	mkm	mkl	mkg
nano	nnm	nnl	nng

SUMMARY OF STENOSCRIPT RULES

1. Write what you hear.

pie	pi	knee	ne

   Write vowel sounds that occur at the beginning or end of a word. Do not write vowel sounds within a word.

animal	anml	borrow	bro

2. When the initial or final sound of a word is the name of a letter of the alphabet, write that letter.

argue	rgu	easy	ez

3. When a base word ends in a double consonant sound, write the first of the two sounds. (Other rules involving consonants take precedence over this rule.)

adopt	adp	text	tx

4. Whenever *d* or *ed* (pronounced *ed* or *duh*) is added to a base word, underline the last letter or symbol.

fixed	fx̲	borrowed	bro̲

5. A plural word ending in *s* or *es* is written with a dot (•) under the final letter or symbol in the word. Verbs that form their third-person singular by adding *s* or *es* also have dots.

cigars	sgṛ	runs	rṇ

6. Use special marks to indicate a period, question mark, comma, hyphen, or dash.	period	\	parentheses	( )
	question mark	?	exclamation mark	!
	hyphen	=	dash	==
	comma	,		
Indicate new paragraphs by two long slant marks.	new paragraph	//		
To indicate capitalization, place tick marks under the last letter or symbol in the word.	Betty	bt (=)	American	amrkn (=)
7. Any common abbreviation that is shorter than the Stenoscript form may be used.	manager	mgr	dollar	$
Write figures for numbers. However, very large rounded numbers are treated as special outlines.	500	5h	8,000	8t
	five	5	three billion	3b
8. Memorize the Stenoscript high-frequency words.	See pages 147–148.			
9. When you hear the *ch* sound, write a small *c*.	chop	cp	teacher	tcr
10. Use a dash to represent the word *the* and the *th* (pronounced *ith*), *nd*, *nt*, *mand*, *mend*, and *ment* sounds.	the	—	bath	b—
	kind	k—	sent	s—
	demand	d—	amend	a—
	cement	s—		

11. When you hear the *ng* sound, write a small g.	angle	agl	eating	elg
12. When you hear the *shun, chun,* or *zhun* sound, write a small *j*.	action	akj	digestion	djsj
	occasion	okj		
13. When you hear the *sh* (pronounced *ish*) or *zh* sound, write a small *z*.	fish	fz	measure	mzr
14. When you hear the *nk* (pronounced *ink*) or *qu* (pronounced *kw*) sound, write a small *q*.	bank	bq	quit	ql
15. Write the letter *l* if it occurs between two vowels. Otherwise, omit the letter *l*.	clever	Kvr	told	ld
16. Write the letter *r* if it occurs between two vowels. Otherwise, omit the letter *r*.	farmer	fmr	truck	lk
17. Use a slant mark (/) to represent the *rd, rt,* and *rk* sounds and the letter group *ward*.	guard	g/	alert	al/
	dark	d/	backward	bk/
18. When you hear the *ry* and *rry* (pronounced *ree*) letter groups at the end of words or the *oi* sound, write a small *y*.	battery	bly	annoy	any

19. When you hear the *mis* or *im* sound at the beginning of a word, write a small *m*.	misfit	mft	image	mj
20. When you hear the *dis* or *des* sound at the beginning of a word, write a small *d*.	discuss	dks	discard	dk/
21. Use special abbreviations for the salutation and complimentary closing of a letter.	See page 154.			
22. When the final single consonant sound of a base word is preceded by a long-vowel sound, write the vowel sound but drop the final consonant sound.	alone	alo	vote	vo
However, when the final consonant is a *j*, *v* or *z* sound, write those sounds instead of the long-vowel sound.	cage	kj	leave	lv
	rose	rz		
23. For words ending in the sounds of *ar*, *er*, *or*, and *ur*, drop the final *r* and write the vowel sound.	fair	fa	here	he
	roar	ro	pure	pu
24. When you hear the *st* sound, write a capital S.	stop	Sp	test	tS

25. Memorize the 30 brief forms.	See page 149.			
26. When you hear the *com, con, contra,* or *counter* sound at the beginning of a word, write a small *k*.	compact	kpk	confirm	kfm
	counteract	kak	contradict	kdk
27. When you hear the *enter, inter, intra,* or *intro* sound at the beginning of a word, write a capital *N*.	intramural	Nmrl	introduce	Ndu
	entering	Ng	interview	Nvu
28. When you hear the *ble* (*bul*) sound at the end of a word, just add a capital *B*.	able	aB	symbol	smB
29. Use a comma (,) to represent the *nce* or *nse* sound at the end of a word.	chance	c,	intense	nt,
30. When you hear the *eeus, shul,* or *shus* sound, write a small *x*.	devious	dvx	facial	fx
	spacious	spx		
31. When you hear the *sub* sound, write a small s.	submit	smt	sublet	slt
32. When you hear the *ad* (pronounced *add*) sound at the beginning of a word, write a small *a*.	admit	amt	admire	amr
33. When you hear the *circ* or *circum* sound, write a capital *C*.	circle	Cl	circumvent	Cv

34. When you hear the *tive* letter-group, write a small *v*.	positive	pzv	relative	rlv
35. When you hear the *lee* sound at the end of a word, write a small letter *l*.	rapidly	rpdl	family	fml
When you hear the *blee* sound at the end of a word, write *Bl*.	possibly	psBl		
36. When you hear the *ful* or *fully* sound, write a capital *F*.	full	F	carefully	kaF
37. When you hear the *un* sound at the beginning of a word, write a small *u*.	unable	uaB	unnecessary	unssy
38. When you hear the *trans* sound at the beginning of a word, write a capital *T*.	transact	Tak	transport	Tp
39. When you hear the *ow* sound, write a small *w*.	how	hw	loud	lwd
40. Memorize the Stenoscript abbreviations for times of day and directions.	See page 153.			